SECRETS *of* SPIRIT COMMUNICATION

About the Authors

Trish MacGregor is the author of dozens of novels and non-fiction books, and she co-authored the Sydney Omarr series of astrology books with her husband, Rob. Trish also teaches workshops on astrology and tarot. She lives in southern Florida.

Robert MacGregor is a New York Times bestselling author of twenty novels and eighteen non-fiction books in the New Age field. His novel *The Prophecy Rock* won the Edgar Allan Poe Award for mystery writing. He has worked with George Lucas, Peter Benchley, and Billy Dee Williams, and has been the subject of many articles. MacGregor also has researched anomalous phenomena for many of his books, including seven *Indiana Jones* sagas and two remote viewing novels. He resides in southern Florida.

SECRETS *of* SPIRIT COMMUNICATION

TECHNIQUES *for* TUNING IN *&* MAKING CONTACT

TRISH MACGREGOR
AND
ROB MACGREGOR

Llewellyn Worldwide
Woodbury, Minnesota

FIRST EDITION
Second Printing, 2020

Book design by Bob Gaul
Cover design by Ellen Lawson
Editing by Rhiannon Nelson

Llewellyn Publications is a registered trademark of Llewellyn Worldwide Ltd.

Library of Congress Cataloging-in-Publication Data
The Library of Congress has already cataloged an earlier printing under LCCN: 2018030930

Llewellyn Worldwide Ltd. does not participate in, endorse, or have any authority or responsibility concerning private business transactions between our authors and the public.

All mail addressed to the author is forwarded, but the publisher cannot, unless specifically instructed by the author, give out an address or phone number.

Any Internet references contained in this work are current at publication time, but the publisher cannot guarantee that a specific location will continue to be maintained. Please refer to the publisher's website for links to authors' websites and other sources.

Llewellyn Publications
A Division of Llewellyn Worldwide Ltd.
2143 Wooddale Drive
Woodbury, MN 55125-2989
www.llewellyn.com

Printed in the United States of America

Contents

Practices

With much love
to our daughter, Megan

And many thanks to all of you
who shared your stories and experiences

Introduction

From ethereal beings to handsome leading men playing ghosts, most of us have some concept of what a spirit is. One of the most common ideas is that spirits haunt and generate fear.

While many popular depictions of spirits are frightening or evil, the spirit of spirit communication is generally benevolent, and comforting. It's an affirmation that our loved ones who have passed on are watching out for us and are able to provide information, insight, and guidance.

Spontaneous Spirit Contact

When spirit contact initially happens spontaneously, particularly in young children, it often paves the way for a lifetime of exploration where the individual learns to use tools for initiating spirit communication.

When Leiny was a young child in Colombia, her dead grandmother often visited her at night. Sometimes she would sit at the end of Leiny's bed, talking to her, or would drift around her room like smoke, a translucent, amorphous form that sang softly. When Leiny told her Catholic parents about these experiences, they became fearful and concerned, and called in a priest who performed an exorcism on the house, on Leiny's bedroom, and on her.

She's now a thirty-nine-year-old mother of two, married to an American who is skeptical about anything connected to spirit communication. She routinely requests help and guidance from spirits when she meditates. She then looks for signs in the ordinary world that her request has been heard.

"I'm the *exception* in my family," she says. "It caused me a lot of pain when I was younger, a feeling of rejection, that I was somehow strange or abnormal. But at this point in my life, I've accepted that. I am who I am." Now she considers contact comforting and supportive.

And Leiny is in good company.

Charles Lindbergh, after flying solo for twenty-two hours over the Atlantic, fighting fatigue and inclement weather, was forced to fly so low he could feel the spray from the whitecaps. That was when his plane filled with what he described as "ghostly presences—vaguely outlined forms, transparent, moving, riding weightless with me in the plane." [1] They advised him on his flight, discussed navigational problems, and reassured him. Years later, Lindbergh wrote, "I've never believed in apparitions, but how can I explain the forms I carried with me through so many hours of this day?" [2]

This type of spirit communication generally occurs when an individual's life is at risk. It's not known if Lindbergh consciously attempted spirit communication after his experience, but it certainly changed his beliefs about what is possible.

While treating a female patient with hypnosis, author and psychiatrist Brian Weiss was shocked and skeptical when the woman began recalling past-life traumas that seemed to hold the key to her recurring nightmares and anxiety attacks. His skepticism vanished when she started acting as a "conduit of information from highly evolved 'spirit

---

1   Charles Lindbergh and Reeve Lindbergh. *The Spirit of St. Louis* (New York: Scribner, 2003), 389.

2   Ibid, 467.

entities"[3] that contained remarkable information about life after death and about Weiss's family and his dead son. This spontaneous experience prompted Weiss to write *Many Lives, Many Masters*, and dramatically altered the course of his life.

The Basics of Contact

Maybe you've experienced spontaneous spirit contact. It was unexpected and surprising, and led you to exploring the possibility that you can generate such contact. While we will provide numerous methods and practices throughout the book, it's best to understand the basics of contact at the outset. Here are several essential steps allowing you to become an active participant in spirit contact.

1. *Recognition*: Undoubtedly, the first step for anyone interested in spirit contact is to recognize that such contact is possible. For some, that's a big step. Examine your own beliefs. If your religious upbringing causes you to believe that such contact is dangerous or evil, then it's likely these fears will interfere with your efforts to make contact. Likewise, if your logical or analytical mind firmly rejects the possibility that spirits can contact the living or that you can initiate such contact, then the likelihood of success is minimized. No doubt the best way to recognize the reality of spirit contact is through your own experiences that you might've dismissed in the past as mere coincidence. Another way is through reading contact stories told by others and noticing how they came to recognize the reality of contact.

2. *Awareness*: Once you have recognized that spirit contact is possible, then you need to increase your awareness of the many ways that such contact can manifest. In other words, the ethereal

---

3   Brian L. Weiss, M.D. *Many Lives, Many Masters—20th Anniversary Edition* (New York: Touchstone Publishing, 2010), 10.

appearance of a lost loved one is but one way that contact might happen. Other senses, including hearing, touch, and smell, could come into play. Other possibilities: signs such as the timely playing of a particular song on the radio or the appearance of an object that reminds you of a lost loved one. Awareness of meaningful coincidences is key.

3. *Intention:* Spontaneous contact can be fulfilling, but even better is when you initiate the contact yourself. That's where intention comes into play. You take the initiative to make contact. Make your request. You might repeat it to yourself or aloud. Maybe you type it on your computer, print it out, and display it where you will see it.

4. *Attention:* Now that you've set your intention, give it attention. Add desire. Visualize the one you want to contact, replay a good memory related to the person now in spirit. You want this experience to manifest.

5. *No tension:* Let it go. Release it. You've done what you needed to do. Now just maintain your awareness, watching for signs. Keep in mind that while you initiated the request for contact, your actions could actually be the result of a nudge from the other side, from a loved one who wants to make contact.

Ways of Spirit Contact

Since we started our blog on synchronicity nine years ago, we have written several thousand posts on every aspect of this phenomenon and received more than thirty thousand comments. Since death is the ultimate mystery we all face, spirit communication has generated an overwhelming and unprecedented interest. So many individuals have shared their experiences on the blog, in private e-mails, and in person that we have amassed a database on spirit communication. It has enabled us to identify the archetypal patterns that ordinary people experience and the specific methods—the secrets—that individuals use to converse with the deceased.

Every day, spirits communicate with ordinary people, usually the loved ones they left behind, but also with strangers. They do this by using anything they can to seize our attention—sounds and scents, objects, places, patterns, dreams and visions, signs and symbols, animals, clusters of numbers, names, birth dates. You don't have to be a medium to converse with them. You don't need a medium to interpret what they say. The language of the dead is synchronicity and you can, in fact, avail yourself of this secret language with simple, effective methods.

You might be thinking of your deceased father, for instance, wishing he were still alive, and suddenly catch the scent of pipe tobacco wafting through your room. Your dad used to smoke a pipe. This mysterious synchronicity, conveyed through a scent, not only seizes your attention, but provides comfort and reassurance that your father's spirit is alive and well in the afterlife and may be reaching out to you.

Or, suppose that while you're thinking of your deceased mother, you tell her to give you a sign that she is okay. Perhaps you even speak to her out loud. You might leave for work and set the intention that the next thing you hear will be your mother communicating with you. In the car, you turn on the radio and the first song you hear is about a mother reaching out to a lost daughter. Goose bumps erupt on your arms. You're struck by the sheer odds that out of all the songs that exist, this one plays in the immediate aftermath of your request. Time and again in our research into spirit communication, we have found that synchronicity, or meaningful coincidence, plays a vital role. We'll explore synchronicity and its relationship to spirit contact in greater depth in chapter 1.

Signs and symbols are another way that spirits let us know of their presence in our lives. A sign could appear in a name. For example, you could meet three people in a week all with a form of the same name—the name of a deceased friend or family member. That would be a sign. A symbol might be the repeated appearance of a particular cloud shape or formation, an image of particular significance to you and someone you wish to contact on the other side. We'll go into details of signs and symbols in chapter 2.

Objects that spirits use to communicate seem to be whatever is most convenient and immediate. From our research and in stories we've heard, they range from white feathers to books, straight pins to coins, mirrors and televisions, text messages, photographs and numbers, and even cake! We'll delve into how objects serve as vehicles for communication with the dead in chapter 3.

Sometimes, communication with spirits involves sounds—voices, whispers, knocking, music, the shattering of glass, and even explosions. On August 11, 2015, author Whitley Strieber lost his wife and creative partner, Anne, to whom he'd been married for forty-five years. We have known the Striebers since our book *The 7 Secrets of Synchronicity* was published in 2010 and they invited us to be guests on their podcast *Dreamland*. We've appeared on the show a number of times since then, have been interviewed by both of them, and became friends. So when we heard of Anne's death on August 12, 2015, Trish immediately wrote Whitley about how sorry we were to hear the news. We had great affection for Anne and admired her wry sense of humor and her profound knowledge of paranormal topics.

Whitley replied that the last several months had been particularly difficult, with Anne bedridden and unable to do anything for herself. But her death, he said, had been peaceful. As Trish wrote back, she silently asked Anne to communicate in some way that might offer Whitley comfort and reassurance. *If we can do anything to help out, Whitley, please let us know.* Just as she typed that last word, *know,* there was a brilliant flash of light and a tremendous explosion in our family room, which is directly off of our offices. The explosion sounded like a transformer does when it blows, except it was inside the house, within a few feet of our respective office doorways.

We shot to our feet, certain the air conditioning or TV had blown out—even though the TV wasn't on. Our dog, who had been stretched out on the couch, leaped to the floor. There wasn't any blackout or brownout in the electrical power. Rob turned on the TV to make sure it still worked. It did. We checked the entire house but didn't find anything broken or blown, not even a light bulb.

Since this happened at the precise moment Trish was typing the word *know* in an e-mail to Whitley, we decided it could be Anne, making her presence *known*.

Trish finished her email to Whitley, describing what had happened. *Anne is already stirring things up on the other side!*

He quickly replied: *She sure as hell is. She is here, you better believe it!*

We've experienced things like this in the past, but never something this immediate, mind-blowing, and synchronous. It seemed that Anne Strieber, whose presence in physical reality was so transformative, was now a force to be reckoned with on the other side. She answered Trish's request in a powerful way. In chapter 4, we'll talk about contact related to sounds and scents.

Animals can also play a role in contact with the other side. Take the story of Denise Williams, who lost her five-year-old daughter Pamela in 2015 to cancer. While Pamela was alive, her parents often noticed the presence of robins when she was outside, and they came to associate robins with Pamela. In the aftermath of her death, they also noticed the brightly colored birds around her grave when they visited the graveyard in Roswell, Georgia.

In March, on the second anniversary of Pamela's death, something startling and awesome happened. A robin was perched on Pamela's gravestone as Denise approached. She extended her hand and it flew onto her index finger. She managed to take a video of the bird while on her hand and the astonishing video had more than three million views in the first week. We'll delve into the world of animals and spirit contact in chapter 5.

Clusters or recurring synchronicities often happen when we need to be reminded that the deceased are always with us and ready to communicate. They are often triggered by intense desire and need. For Debra, a cluster involving a particular date was especially meaningful. In 1993, she gave birth to her second daughter, Laryssa. The baby was born with a spontaneous genetic mutation and was given just twelve days to live. But Laryssa beat the odds and lived for nearly two years. During that time, Debra and her husband, Larry, met many helpful people from the local hospice who provide home care for Laryssa. She died on October 9, 1995.

Twelve years later, Debra and Larry desperately searched for a physician who could treat Debra's chronic immune disorder. They found a doctor who was supposedly the best in the San Diego area. The day of her appointment, the doctor read through Debra's medical history and burst out crying. "I know you both. I worked with Laryssa as a volunteer."

Debra suddenly remembered her, too. "We all cried and hugged," Debra recalls. "It was very emotional." The doctor told them she had a daughter who was born on October 9, 1995, the very day Laryssa died. "We were stunned by the synchronicity." Debra and Larry felt as if their daughter's spirit had reached out to them, reminding them that help and guidance are always available from our deceased loved ones. We'll look more into cluster communication in chapter 6.

We spend much of our time thinking and acting, thinking and acting. Our minds and bodies are busily involved in the everyday world. But the constant babble of our thoughts as we multitask our way through the day not only can create excessive stress, but is also not a viable environment for spirit contact. It's important to set aside time for relaxation, meditation or self-hypnosis, automatic writing, channeling, and other practices that allow us to enter an altered state of consciousness. Doing so allows us to increase our awareness of the many ways that spirits contact us, and provides a state of mind conducive to making contact. In chapter 7, we explore altered states and their relationship to spirit contact. When we dream, we bypass our logical minds and merge with our intuitive nature, and that enhances our chances to make spirit contact. In the ancient practice of dream incubation, you "plant a seed" in your mind before going to sleep. It's not only a means of initiating contact, but is also a way of seeking guidance from the other side or solutions to specific issues.

When Rob's mother developed dementia and could no longer live alone, he searched for facilities that could accommodate her. He narrowed their choices to two places. Both had pros and cons. He incubated a dream in which he asked for guidance from his deceased father. In the dream, his father handed him two checks for small amounts of money. Rob's interpretation of the dream was that they should choose the less-expensive facility, so that's what he did. His mother toured the facility, loved it, and has since moved in. We'll provide specific methods for inducing contact through dreams in chapter 8.

In the American Southwest, petroglyphs that date from 3000 BC to AD 1 often depict the existence and intervention of the spirit world in human affairs.[4] Shamanism, which has existed in some form since mankind first appeared on the planet, not only readily acknowledges the existence of spirits but provides techniques for entering their world and communicating with them. We'll take a look at shamanism and how it's linked to spirit contact in chapter 9.

We were walking along a heavily forested trail after dark in the Dominican Republic with an American we'd met named Jason. Chirring choruses of frogs and insects accompanied us. The tropical night

---

4   Joe Zentner. "Petroglyphs and Pictographs." *DesertUSA,* https://www.desertusa
    .com/desert-activity/desert-rock-art.html.

sounds were so loud that they almost drowned out our conversation. Jason was curious about the type of books we wrote and told us he was a science-oriented person and didn't believe in anything that hinted at the paranormal. He considered it a distraction that leads people away from following logic and the laws of science.

We didn't want to start an argument so Rob made a comment about our sonorous accompaniment. "Do you remember those old black-and-white vampire and werewolf movies where someone would be walking through a dark forest when suddenly all the night sounds would abruptly stop and you knew that meant the creature was ready to attack?" At that moment, before Trish or Jason could respond, the chorus went silent. Every creature abruptly halted their trilling and croaking. We glanced at each other and hurried along the trail until we reached a road, streetlights, and hotels. Jason had no response when we told him that was a synchronicity—actually, a trickster synchronicity. We saw Jason a couple more times during our stay, but he didn't speak to us again. The trickster has that effect sometimes.

Many of us are so wrapped up in the everyday world of cause and effect that we ignore our essential spiritual nature, and the idea that reality is more expansive than we might presume. That's when we experience startling incidents filled with irony, like what happened on that trail. In chapter 10, we'll delve into the archetype of the trickster and its role in contact with the other side.

Your Beliefs

Keep a journal for the practices in this book. You might start out by jotting down your beliefs about the afterlife. Talk about it with family and friends. Find out how your views differ from other people's. If you follow a traditional religion, how does its tenets about life after death relate to your own? Be aware that any exploration of contact may lead you to change any assumptions or suppositions about the afterlife.

Polling on the Afterlife

Skeptics tend to dismiss experiences like those we describe in this book as wishful thinking, a silly hope that the consciousness of the deceased is still alive somewhere. After all, consensus reality is quick to tell us that when you die, you're dead, and that's the end of the story, the end of the road. Yet in polls conducted over the years about a belief in the afterlife, the majority of respondents claim to believe in a heaven, but exactly what that means is up for grabs. *Huffington Post* cited a 2014 CBS News poll where three out of four Americans believed in either heaven or hell. "Sixty-six percent of respondents said they believed in both heaven and hell, 11% in heaven only, and 17% in neither. Americans who don't identify with any particular religion or are atheist or agnostic are much less likely to say they believe in either heaven or hell. Just under half say they believe in neither, while 36% believe in both and 7% in heaven only. In a 2013 Pew poll, 27% of agnostics and 13% of atheists said they believed in some kind of afterlife."[5]

Yet in this same article, it's stated that in recent polls, nearly "one in five Americans expressed belief in reincarnation, a proportion that has stayed roughly at the same level since the question was first asked in 1968. In the 2011 poll, 15% of Protestants and 24% of Catholics said they believed in reincarnation."

In other words, beliefs and opinions about the afterlife are all over the place and are influenced heavily by a person's religious or spiritual beliefs. But the bottom line is that *we don't know what happens when we die.* We have spiritual and religious systems whose platforms spell it out, but how do we know any of it is true? Our only gauge is how we *feel* about these various belief systems—how we sift and sort, pick and choose—according to our own life experiences.

---

5   Kathleen Weldon. "Paradise Polled: Americans and the Afterlife." http://www .huffingtonpost.com/kathleen-weldon/paradise-polled-americans_b_7587538.html.

About Us

We've investigated spirit contact through firsthand experiences as well as through research. Over the years, we've gathered numerous stories on our synchronicity blog that feature astonishing encounters and meaningful coincidences related to deceased loved ones. We've also explored spirit communication as a facet of synchronicity in our books *7 Secrets of Synchronicity, Synchronicity and the Other Side,* and *The Synchronicity Highway.*

We want you to know that regardless of your age, gender, spiritual beliefs, ethnicity, or cultural background, spirit communication is accessible to all of us. Your exploration will be facilitated by the methods we describe. And who knows what you may find. Whether you're just curious or would like to communicate with loved ones you have lost, we invite you to join us on this exploration. Initially, it may feel as exotic as a trip to the heart of the Amazon rainforest. But once you become accustomed to the terrain, you'll discover that the dead have wisdom, advice, and guidance to impart and that your contact with them enriches your life immeasurably.

1

The ABCs of Synchronicity

SYNCHRONICITY INVOLVING SPIRIT contact often shocks and surprises us, and seizes our attention so completely that we're forced to pause and reconsider our notions about how things work. We're left with a sense of wonder and bewilderment about who or what is orchestrating events because it certainly seems something larger is at work.

In the spring of 2013, it was obvious that our elderly cat, Tigerlily, was reaching the end of her life. We'd had her since 1997, a gray tabby who once had ruled the roost, but could now barely make it out of the kitchen. She had trouble eating and would occasionally start choking, but we figured that as long as she could eat something and didn't appear in pain, we wouldn't intervene.

On the morning of June 4 that year, Trish gave her some Cheerios in milk, mixed in well-squashed sardines, and Tigerlily ate what she could. When Trish later went into the kitchen, Tigerlily was foraging in the cabinet where the cat food is kept and glanced around at her. She emitted a soft, pathetic meow and Trish realized she was starving to death. A bib of milk and food covered her snout and chest that reminded Trish of her dad in his final days, when the mere act of lifting a fork to his mouth was nearly impossible. Trish knew it was time.

On the way to the vet's office, Tigerlily sat in a carrier in the passenger seat, mewing softly. Trish remembered her dad describing how he had felt when he'd driven his and her mother's cat—Tigger, another gray-striped tabby—to the vet to be euthanized. She remembered the pain in her dad's voice, the anguish he'd felt, and asked him to tell her if she was doing the right thing. She voiced her request out loud and because her need for confirmation was so strong, she felt sure her dad would give her a sign.

But by the time she arrived at the vet's office fifteen minutes later, the only thing that had happened was a deepening of her own anxiety. She was visibly upset when she walked into the vet's office. On the sign-in sheet, Trish entered Tigerlily's name and next to *reason for visit*, she wrote: *needs to be put to sleep.*

One of the vet's assistants came over with a box of Kleenex and crouched down beside her. "Listen," she said quietly. "A friend of mine had a near-death experience several years ago. When she returned, she was psychic and could see spirits—of humans and animals. Tigerlily will be back."

In the examining room, the on-duty vet explained that Tigerlily would be sedated first, then put to sleep. "I did a double take when I saw your cat's name," he said.

"Why?" Trish asked.

"Well, a couple days ago one of our employees rushed in with a wounded kitten. We fixed her broken leg, but had to amputate one of her other legs to save her. She's doing fine now. I named her Tigerlily."

The stunning synchronicity seemed to be the message from Trish's dad she asked for. She looked at the vet, managing to stammer, "Wow. That's an uplifting coincidence. Thank you for that."

"Hey," he said softly, passing her a box of Kleenex. "They come into life and they leave life. You're doing the right thing. Seventeen is a long life for a cat."

Trish stayed with Tigerlily as she slipped into unconsciousness, stroking her, whispering to her, reassuring her that all the other animals we'd lost over the years would be there to greet her and that she would be back. When she took her last breath, the vet took a mold of her front paw and said they would mail it when it was ready. It arrived two days later with her paw print and named etched into it.

This kind of synchronicity, falling so closely to Trish's request to her dad, defies the odds. Of all the names that might have been given to the kitten whose leg had been amputated, it was Tigerlily—not Tiger, not Lily, not Tigerlilly with two Ls, but *Tigerlily*. For Trish, the synchronicity wasn't just comforting. It felt as if Tigerlily herself had reached out to Trish as she was dying and the vet—and Trish's dad—had been her voice: *They come into life and they leave life.*

Synchronicity is a kind of alchemy that transforms us or a decision we're making in an essential way. The alchemy occurs because of what the synchronicity says to you, its impact on you.

This was certainly the case for Carl Jung during a visit in the 1950s with Henry Fierz, a chemistry professor with whom he had become friends over the years. Friez had dropped by at five o'clock one afternoon to talk to Jung about a manuscript by a scientist who had recently died. Fierz felt the manuscript should be published, but Jung, who had read it, thought otherwise. Their debate about the manuscript apparently became somewhat heated and at one point, Jung glanced at his watch, as if he were about to dismiss Friez. Then he seemed puzzled by the time and explained that his watch had just been returned from the repair shop, but it read five o'clock, the time Friez had arrived.

Jung asked Friez the time: it was 5:35. As Richard Tarnas recounted in *Psyche and Cosmos: Intimations of a New World View,* Jung apparently said, "So you have the right time, and I have the wrong time. Let us discuss the thing again." In the ensuing discussion, Friez convinced Jung the manuscript should be published. "Here, the synchronistic event is of interest not because of its intrinsic coincidental forces, but because of the meaning Jung drew from it, essentially using it as a basis for challenging and redirecting his own conscious attitude," Tarnas wrote. [6]

Many of us might not draw a correlation between a stopped watch and a discussion. But synchronicity, by definition, is the coming together of similar inner and outer events in a way that is meaningful to the individual and can't be explained by cause and effect. This means that the outer world—and all of nature and our surroundings—can carry meaning just as the inner world does. Jung, who was accustomed to perceiving and thinking symbolically, recognized the synchronicity and changed his thinking accordingly.

Tarnas noted in *Cosmos and Psyche* that Jung recognized all events as "sources of potential and spiritual significance." It didn't matter to him whether they originated from human consciousness or from the "larger matrix of the world" because he saw nature and a person's surrounding environment as a living template of "potential synchronistic meaning that could illuminate the human sphere. He attended to sudden or unusual movements or appearances of animals, flocks of birds, the wind, storms, the sudden louder lapping of the lake outside the window of his consulting room … as possible symbolic relevance for the parallel unfolding of interior psychological realities." [7]

In other words, Jung used everything in his environment as potential signs and symbols. It seems that once you recognize coincidence as meaningful, once you're in the flow of it, the inner self and the larger outer matrix chatter constantly to each other. We only have to listen.

---

6   Richard Tarnas. *Cosmos and Psyche: Intimations of a New World View.* (New York: Penguin Group, 2006), 54.

7   Ibid., 56.

These startling events often happen near the time of death of a loved one, as in the following case.

Connecting with Coincidence

Bernard Beitman, a visiting professor of psychiatry at the University of Virginia (UVA), is the first psychiatrist since Jung to undertake a serious study of synchronicity. His interest, his passion, was initially triggered by an experience with spontaneous spirit contact similar to that of Leiny, Weiss, and Lindbergh, whom we wrote about in the introduction.

It began on February 27, 1973, at 11 p.m. when Beitman, then thirty-one, suddenly found himself bent over the kitchen sink in his apartment in San Francisco, choking on something that had caught in his throat. "I couldn't cough it up. I hadn't eaten anything. I didn't know what was in my throat."

After about fifteen minutes, he could finally breathe and swallow normally. The next day, on his birthday, his brother called to tell him their father had died in Wilmington, Delaware, at 2 a.m. Eastern Standard Time. Beitman was three thousand miles and three time zones away, so 2 a.m. Eastern was 11 p.m. in San Francisco. His father had bled out in his throat and choked on his own blood at about the same time Beitman was choking uncontrollably.

"Was this just coincidence?" Beitman writes in *Connecting with Coincidence: The New Science for Using Synchronicity and Serendipity in Your Life.* [8] "No. The timing was too perfect. The experience was too visceral. I loved my father, but I had no idea that our connection could transcend time and space in this way. I began to wonder if other people had had similar experiences."

---

8 Bernard D. Beitman. *Connecting with Coincidence: The New Science for Using Synchronicity and Serendipity in Your Life.* (Deerfield Beach, FL: HCI Books, 2016), 2.

He discovered that his experience was not unique and it launched his research into synchronicity. What's particularly interesting about Beitman's journey is that as an academic, he risks ridicule from peers, derision from skeptics, and all the usual dismissive comments that are hurled at people in the academic world who stray from the consensus.

However, he teaches in the same university where Dr. Ian Stevenson taught. Stevenson was also a psychiatrist and his research area was reincarnation, with forays into precognition, telepathy, and other paranormal topics avoided by most academics. Beitman, in fact, belongs to a small group of UVA professors and researchers that included Stevenson before his death, who meet monthly to share ideas and discuss these outlier topics. So it seems that UVA encourages their professors to think outside the box.

A story Beitman relates on the first page of his book is clearly an instance of spirit communication. A woman named Saundra was eating Chinese food at her dad's place and texted her sister that one of their favorite movies, *The Wizard of Oz*, was on TV. Her sister replied that she recalled watching that movie with their mom, who was deceased, and that their mother would always fix popcorn. While Saundra was reading her sister's text message, she popped open a fortune cookie. What did the fortune say? *Popcorn.*

Saundra, surprised and stunned, texted this development to her sister. "They both felt the presence and comfort of their mother,"[9] Beitman writes. This kind of childhood memory about their mom undoubtedly created an intense emotional desire for communication with her and may have triggered the spontaneous and nearly immediate contact.

Over the years, we've cracked open a lot of fortune cookies and have never seen the word *popcorn*. Again, what are the odds? How many words are there in the English language? When you do a search on the Internet with this question, the range of words extends from the Oxford

---

9   Ibid., 2.

Dictionary's estimate of a quarter of a million *distinct* words to the 2014 estimate by the Global Language Monitor of 1,025,109. Whichever figure you choose results in astronomical odds that Saundra's fortune cookie would include the very word that she and her sister were texting about. And these huge odds are one of the first things that synchronicities involving spirit communication usually have in common.

Even Beitman's choking experience, which happened at the same time his father choked to death, defies the odds. After all, he might have experienced any number of things at that moment—vivid memories of his father, fear, anxiety. But his experience was physical, alarming, and so shocking in light of what he learned the next day from his brother that it launched his research.

This is how synchronicity works, particularly when it involves loved ones who are dying or who have already passed on. Beitman could have ignored the coincidence. Trish could have written off the synchronicity concerning Tigerlily as an interesting but random coincidence. But these experiences often leave an indelible impression that urges us to dig a little deeper, to explore, to figure it out. And once we answer that call to a mysterious exploration, our lives are forever changed. That's what happened to Darren of Brisbane, Australia, in 2006.

Sylvester the Cat

Darren's experience also involved a cat, a black-and-white tuxedo male named Sylvester. Sylvester always liked to sleep in the road in front of Darren's house, so it wasn't surprising when one day he was killed by a car. The woman who hit Sylvester moved his body from the road to a footpath that led to the house. Darren and his wife were grocery shopping when it happened and found Sylvester's body when they arrived home that evening. Since it was too late for Darren to bury Sylvester, he put his body in a box so he could bury him the next day.

The next morning, Darren got out his shovel and started digging in his backyard. The ground was so hard he couldn't dig more than six inches before striking rock. He decided to instead bury Sylvester in the woods a few miles from where he lived. He found a burial spot in the trees, in softer ground.

He turned on his car's radio and began digging. When the hole was deep enough so wild animals couldn't get to Sylvester's body, he placed the cat inside and said his goodbyes. As he shoveled dirt over Sylvester, the radio started playing Peter Gabriel's "Digging in the Dirt."

"I was beside myself, thinking of all the songs that could have come on the radio. How appropriate it was, this one. Whenever I hear that song I always think back to that day of digging in the dirt and saying farewell to my little pal."

What are the odds this song played as Darren buried his cat? Probably astronomical. It made a tremendous impact on him and awakened such a deep awareness in Darren about synchronicity that he now blogs about it.

PRACTICE 1: HOW RECEPTIVE ARE YOU?

Let's say a friend confides that she has been in touch with her father, who recently passed away, and claims it has happened multiple times. She describes the contact as a particular song that was her father's favorite. One morning, it was the first thing she heard when she turned on her car radio. When she walked into a clothing shop one day, the same song was playing. When she was in the bookstore, a book about the musician who sings the song fell at her feet.

What's your reaction? What's the first thought that goes through your mind? Check the statements that fit your reaction.

1. Grieving has unhinged her.

2. Grieving has made her imagine things.

3. She's looking for answers in all the wrong places.

4. When you're dead, you're dead. There's no afterlife.

5. You're intrigued and ask questions about her experiences.

6. You urge her to write about these experiences, to record them in some way.

7. You want to know how she feels when she experiences these things.

8. You ask if there are any other clusters like this that she has experienced.

If you checked any of the first four, then your receptivity is at rock bottom. You may want to read up on near-death experiences that document what people see and hear when they are clinically dead. This book is a good place to start. If you checked any of the last four, then you are wide open to spirit contact. Get ready to learn more!

Why Do Spirits Communicate?

For many of us, contact with the spirit world initially happens spontaneously without any effort on our part. Often that contact involves synchronicity. Only later do we consider taking action to make it happen. So why do those on the other side seek out contact with us?

One of the most likely reasons spirits reach out is to alert loved ones in the physical world that existence continues. *Hey, we're still here. You just can't see us with your five senses now.* Perhaps they hope to raise awareness. Or to finish a matter they weren't able to complete while alive. But probably the number one reason spirits make contact is to comfort those left behind and assure them they are okay, that there is no reason to mourn them. In fact, excessive feelings of loss might make it more difficult for the deceased to move on to a higher plane of existence.

Archetypes & Storytelling

Carl Jung, who coined the term *synchronicity*, was such an atypical psychiatrist for the time in which he lived that he never went through psychoanalysis himself. Instead, as Deirdre Bair, author of *Jung: A Biography*, notes he used his "'personal myth' as the starting point to

formulate what he believed were enduring objective truths. He juxta-
posed his personal myth against the myths of many disparate cultures,
eventually adding new terms to the common vocabulary and new ways
of thinking about ideas." [10]

As a result, he coined two other words in addition to *synchronicity*
that are now part of the lexicon of Western culture: the *collective unconscious* and *archetypes*. The first phrase refers to a kind of psychic reposi-
tory of our history as a species. It contains images Jung called *archetypes*
that are common to all people regardless of nationality, race, gender, cultural background, or religious beliefs. These images are found in folklore
and mythology, fairy tales and fantasies, legends, dreams, and in hallu-
cinations. Mother, father, child, family, wise old man or woman, animal,
hero, trickster, shadow, orphan, victim, quest, separation from parents,
and, of course, birth and death—hose archetypes are the most common.

Archetypes, when used effectively in storytelling, touch us deeply
and tend to stay with us. Take Indiana Jones, the embodiment of the
likeable adventurer and hero archetype, or Luke Skywalker, the young,
innocent hero whose ultimate quest was to defend the universe against
Darth Vader. Vader is the personification of two archetypes—father and
the shadow. Dexter, the name of the character and the Showtime TV
series, was also a shadow archetype, an antihero, one who is haunted by
his dead father who counsels and cajoles him from the other side.

In Alice Sebold's 2002 novel *The Lovely Bones,* a teenage girl is raped
and murdered by a neighbor and from her "personal heaven" keeps tabs
on her family and friends, witnessing how her death impacted their
lives. The novel's large archetypal themes—the death of a child, the survival of consciousness, the fractured family structure—made the book
a bestseller. Peter Jackson directed the film adaptation released in 2009.
Toward the end of the novel and the movie, there's a powerful spirit
communication scene where the spirit of Susie, the murdered teen,

---

10   Deirdre Bair. *Jung: A Biography.* (New York: Little, Brown Company, 2003), 5.

enters the body of her friend, Ruth, while she is with Ray, who had a crush on Susie before she was murdered. Ray senses Susie's presence and when he and Ruth make love, he knows he is making love to Susie.

One of the best movies about spirit communication was the 1990 blockbuster *Ghost*. Sam Wheat, a murdered banker, desperately tries to warn his lover, Molly Jensen, a potter, that his coworker, Carl, is responsible for his murder. Carl needs to obtain Sam's book of passwords so he can access and launder excess money in various bank accounts and figures he can do this by wooing Molly.

Sam learns how to manipulate physical objects from the spirit realm and, several times, these objects divert Molly and save her from danger. But Sam's real break in communicating with Molly comes through Oda Mae Brown, a con artist who claims to be a medium. In the movie version, Whoopi Goldberg played this part. When Oda Mae hears Sam talking to her, she realizes she really *can* hear spirits and from that point forward, she becomes instrumental in communicating with Molly and exposing Carl's plans.

The story has many of the elements common to spirit communication: sounds and noises generated by Sam's spirit, Molly's sense of his presence, a medium with whom he can communicate. And there's a scene at the end similar to one in *The Lovely Bones,* where Oda Mae allows Sam's spirit to inhabit her body so that he and Molly can experience one slow, romantic dance together.

Then there's *The Sixth Sense,* probably M. Night Shyamalan's best film. Bruce Willis plays a child psychiatrist and Haley Joel Osment plays a kid who talks to the spirits of people who don't realize they're dead. Shyamalan nailed the archetypal themes in this movie and in the event you haven't seen it, we won't provide any spoilers. If you're interested in spirit contact, see the movie.

Stories like these capture the archetypes of spirit communication, illustrating how a tragedy ignites our awareness that nothing is what it appears, that there's a deeper order in the universe, and that the language of this hidden order is synchronicity. But in real life, spirit contact is often stranger than fiction.

In 1991, Jenean Gilstrap's brother died under mysterious circumstances while living in Rogers, Arkansas. Some of her best childhood memories were of her and her brother picking and eating figs for hours at a time during the Arkansas summers. She can still recall the sticky feel of the leaves and the figs, and how the summer heat released a richness of scents. She recalls their laughter and what sheer fun and joy it was.

Imagine her surprise when she found fig preserves from Rogers, Arkansas, at a TJ Maxx in Delaware, where she lived.

"Rogers, Arkansas, is a little town in between Bentonville and Springdale, an area where many of our ancestors settled, where there is still family land, and where my brother lived at the time of his death. It holds special significance for me," Jenean said.

Over the July 4th weekend in 2010, Jenean was in her kitchen with her grandson, and asked if he would like to sample some of the new fig preserves. She told her grandson about how she and her brother used to pick them when they were kids. In the midst of their discussion there was a knock at the door. A neighbor popped in to let Jenean know that she had just returned from a farmer's market up the road and saw fresh figs there. It had been at least two years since Jenean had mentioned figs to her neighbor, but the woman had remembered and just happened to stop by while Jenean was talking about figs with her grandson.

Her synchronicity antenna started twitching.

That evening, she clicked on the counter gadget on her blog that provides information about the visitors, including their location. She saw that someone from Rogers, Arkansas, had visited her blog for the first time. And then it hit her. She felt this experience was actual contact with her brother's spirit through two things she would recognize—figs and the place where he had died.

Jenean's wonderful childhood memories of her brother are deeply embedded in her emotional being and may have provided the trigger for contact with her deceased brother. The spirits of our loved ones will use anything they can to communicate with us. But unless we're aware that coincidences are meaningful and we listen to the chatter of synchronicities that rush through the undercurrent of our daily lives, we may miss the message.

Synchronicity & Contact

Synchronicity and spirit communication can occur anytime but are more frequent during pivotal phases of our lives. And nothing is more pivotal than the approach of death, the moment of death, and after death.

When a loved one—human or animal—is approaching death, synchronicities are warnings intended to prepare you. They may be more difficult to interpret if the person or pet isn't ill, but you probably will recognize the significance of the event, whatever it is. Sometimes these things happen in clusters. You might, for instance, have several experiences in a few hours or over a period of days. It's helpful if you interpret these experiences as you might interpret a dream.

Here are some examples of these types of occurrences. They are varied, but convey the same message:

- While on your way to the grocery store, a bird swoops out of the sky and slams into your windshield, breaking its neck. A few days later, a friend is in a car accident and dies of a broken neck.

- While browsing in a bookstore, a book about spirit communication falls at your feet. Shortly afterward, you begin to experience contact with a deceased relative.

- As you're cleaning out your attic, you run across a toy that your favorite aunt gave you when you were a kid. It has split down the middle. Not long afterward, you learn that she has passed on.

- Just as you e-mail your sister about finding an item that belonged to your parents, a pair of hummingbirds touch down on a bush outside your window. You're sure it's your parents attempting to communicate with you.

- Several months after your pet parrot dies, you dream she is alive and well. The next day, a flock of wild parrots lands in your backyard and you feel the dream was an actual communication with your deceased parrot.

PRACTICE 2: YOUR "OUT-OF-THIS-WORLD" SYNCHRONICITY

Do you recall any synchronicities linked to deceased loved ones?

If so, record your experiences in your journal. It's an excellent way of tracking your progress. Be sure to note the date, time, weather conditions, and your own state of mind.

How were you feeling emotionally when the experience occurred? How long did it take for you to recognize the synchronicity?

The most important part of keeping a journal is that the process helps you build awareness of the many ways those on the other side make contact. It enables you to build a database of patterns that are unique to your experiences of spirit contact.

2

❋

Signs &
Symbols

THE SIGNS AND symbols the dead use to communicate with the living
can be tricky things, as idiosyncratic as the spirits themselves. But it's
these very idiosyncrasies that grab our attention and can provide clues
about who may be trying to get in touch.

Signs cover a vast spectrum of possibilities. The ones we have found to
be most common include: objects that held significance to the deceased, a
particular piece of music or song, a book, birth date, a certain cloud pattern, a particular shape that forms on a steamed-up window or mirror, a
cluster of numbers or names, lights and appliances that turn off or on for
no discernible reason. This list is by no means exhaustive. You may find
other signs and symbols that spirits use in communication.

The signs can be so startling and personal that we know immediately that something unusual is happening. But they can also be ordinary and so mundane that we fail to notice them and the moment of
contact sails right past us, unfulfilled. If the spirit is persistent, though,
there will be other attempts, often with the same sign. That was the case
for Charles.

Objects: Pennies from Heaven

Our local dog park is one of those places where synchronicities are just waiting to happen, but it isn't a spot where we expect to hear about spirit communication.

The park-goers who arrive day after day are a pool of diversity. They are young and old and middle-aged, black and white and Latino, Christians and Jews, agnostics and atheists. They are teachers, childcare providers, construction workers, Olympian equestrians, IT experts, artists, and writers. Some are rich, many are middle class, some are poor and struggling. But they all have one thing in common: a love of dogs. It's this commonality that often leads to discussions that veer into unexpected terrain.

One recent Friday afternoon, Trish and Noah, our golden retriever, arrived earlier than usual at the dog park and found the place nearly deserted. Just one other person, a midde-aged man named Charles, was there with his three dogs. He's a winter resident in our South Florida town where he works in the horse industry as a farrier. He started talking about a border collie he and his wife had owned several years earlier. The dog was twelve years old when diagnosed with throat cancer and had to be put down. It devastated both of them, but his wife took it especially hard.

Not long afterward, his wife was diagnosed with throat cancer and died within four months. It was, he admitted, a sad and difficult time. Trish felt compelled to ask Charles if he ever felt his wife around. This isn't a question she usually asks strangers, especially someone who recently has lost a loved one, and she wondered how Charles would react.

"I sense her around all the time."

"In what way?"

"Well, for years, she would often hand me a penny and tell me to keep it in my pocket for good luck. Very soon after her death, I started finding pennies in my car, around the house, in my clothing, in my suitcase when I was traveling." He said he could understand the pennies in his car, loose change that might have dropped out of her purse or my wallet. But the pennies he ran across in the house were in odd spots— the bathroom, the shower, a high shelf. The pennies in his clothing didn't make sense, either. He wasn't in the habit of slipping loose change in his pockets. But it was the pennies in his suitcase that convinced him it was the spirit of his wife, letting him know she was around. "I knew it was her. These were *pennies*, not *quarters*," he said with a quick laugh.

His initial contact with his dead wife was spontaneous, triggered by his grief after her death. But once he was convinced it was possible for them to communicate, he began to look for other signs and symbols. Not long after the pennies started showing up, Charles noticed that whenever he was feeling his wife's absence more than usual, he would see a particular pattern of clouds overhead, always the same pattern. He felt that it was another way she communicated with him.

One day while shoeing horses at a client's barn, the owner said she sensed his wife around. He had heard the owner was an eccentric New Age-type who said she communicated with spirits. Charles smiled and thanked her, assuming she was just trying to comfort him.

Then she said, "She wants to know why you stopped kissing her picture."

Charles was floored. On the wall near his bed were two photos, one of her and the other of the two of them together. Every night before he went to bed, he kissed his fingers and touched the photo of her and wished her good night. But recently, he'd repainted the bedroom and had to take the photos down. So he'd inadvertently stopped kissing his wife good night.

"No one knew this," Charles said. "Not even my closest friends. It's not a real manly thing to do, I guess. So how did this woman know *that?*"

"It sounds like she's a genuine medium," Trish replied. "So has your wife been around recently?"

"That first year after she passed, she was around all the time. The pennies, the cloud patterns. But not so much anymore." He pointed at Georgie, one of his dogs. "But my wife urged me to get her."

In other words, she was around for the important stuff.

Charles could have ignored all those pennies, ignored the cloud patterns, could have written it all off to random coincidences. But once he felt certain that contact was happening, he *encouraged* it, *summoned* it through his desire, *sought* it. The information the mediumistic horse owner provided, which no one else knew, was another level of confirmation.

As Bernard Beitman notes in *Connecting with Coincidence,* "The objects and living creatures in the world around us can supply symbolic reassurances about the people we lose through death." [11]

Reluctance & Ridicule

Part of the challenge with spirit contact in the West is that the main-stream consensus is no one can communicate with the dead. We are taught to doubt our own experiences. Even though this attitude has loosened up somewhat in the past twenty years, people who experience spirit contact are sometimes reluctant to admit it for fear of ridicule.

What would my boss think? I could get fired.

It would freak out my spouse; he (she) doesn't believe in any of this stuff.

My kids might laugh at me.

My parents will think I've gone around the bend.

Please don't use my real name.

I would only discuss this subject on a closed or secret Facebook group site.

11   Bernard D. Beitman. *Connecting with Coincidence: The New Science for Using Synchronicity and Serendipity in Your Life.* (Deerfield Beach, FL: HCI Books, 2016), 123.

When you're afraid of what other people might think about your experience, you tend to attract more of the same type of skepticism— from your church, your minister, your neighbor, spouse, closest friends, kids, from anyone in your environment. So the next time you find yourself reluctant to share your experience, to explore it with someone, ask yourself: What's the worst thing that could happen? Will your spouse divorce you? Will your boss fire you? Will your kids really laugh at you?

Usually, this kind of fear has little or no basis in reality. It's just your inner critic at work, that niggling voice in the back of your head that probably belongs to someone in your childhood who reprimanded you for not being like everyone else. So if you're reluctant to share a spirit contact story out of fear of ridicule, write about it first. Sometimes, that's all it takes to overcome the fear.

Knowing the Unknowable

Awareness and intuition are like conjoined twins when it comes to synchronicity and spirit contact. Without an awareness that coincidence is meaningful and that communication with the dead is possible, your intuition is left screaming in an empty room: *pay attention, look at this, it's important.* In the same way, if your intuition is alerting you that something is happening and your belief system about the survival of consciousness after death is complete skepticism, then the message might never arrive. It's an e-mail that goes directly to spam.

However, if you're skeptical or have never given much thought to the survival of consciousness, the death of someone you love can pivot things quickly and irrevocably. Suddenly, you know the unknowable.

Michael Shermer, the author of *Why People Believe Weird Things: Pseudoscience, Superstition, and Other Confusions of Our Time,* is the founding publisher of *Skeptic* magazine, and the executive director of the Skeptics Society. He's also a monthly columnist for *Scientific American.* In his column on October 1, 2014, Shermer wrote about an experience with synchronicity and spirit contact that apparently drilled into and perhaps even shattered his skeptic's amour. [12]

When he got engaged, his fiancée's belongings were shipped to the United States from Germany, and among them was her grandfather's 1978 transistor radio. Her grandfather had died when she was sixteen and she'd been quite close to him.

The radio had been silent for decades, and Shermer couldn't get it working again. It continued its silence in the back of a desk drawer in the couple's bedroom. In June of 2014, Shermer and his fiancée were married. After the ceremony, his wife confided that she was lonely, missed her family back in Germany, and wished her grandfather could have been alive to give her away. The couple walked to the back of the house where they heard music playing, a love song.

They searched for the source of the music, couldn't find it, and then his wife turned to him with a startled look. "That can't be what I think it is, can it?" she asked.

It was the transistor radio in the drawer. "My grandfather is here with us," she said, tearfully. "I'm not alone."

Shortly before the ceremony had started, Shermer's daughter had heard music coming from the radio. But the couple had been in the room only moments earlier without hearing any music. The radio continued to work through the wedding night.

"Fittingly, it stopped working the next day and has remained silent ever since," Shermer wrote. This experience led Shermer to conclude in his column, "We should not shut the doors of perception when they may be opened to us to marvel in the mysterious."

Some of the most powerful synchronicities occur during peak moments in our lives—birth, death, and marriage, as in Shermer's case.

---

12   Michael Shermer. "Anomalous Events That Can Shake One's Skepticism to the Core." *Scientific American*, Oct. 1, 2014. https://www.scientificamerican.com /article/anomalous-events-that-can-shake-one-s-skepticism-to-the-core/.

For Shermer, the startling event showed that even though anecdotal evidence is not scientific proof, such personal experiences with spirit communication are powerful and not easily dismissed when it happens to you. Considering his reputation as an ardent skeptic and debunker, his column about his experience with life-after-death communication was a bold offering. He is, however, still editor of *Skeptic*.

Many spirit communication experiences initially occur spontaneously and tend to be so weird and in your face they can't be ignored. It's as if this first contact is intended to blow open your awareness so you become an active participant in spirit communication.

The Cultural Influence on Signs & Symbols

There are few losses more tragic and heartbreaking than parents losing a child. As every parent knows, your kids are supposed to outlive *you*. But over the years in our research into synchronicity and spirit contact, we've heard from a number of parents who have lost their children to illness, disease, accidents, and suicide. And usually, signs and symbols of contact occur quickly after death and sometimes persist for years.

In Western culture, the survival of consciousness after death is largely relegated to religious and spiritual traditions, and is typically not a subject deemed worthy of serious study by mainstream science. But Eastern cultures view the subject through a different lens. Survival of consciousness is linked to reincarnation, which is considered a fact of life as well as a religious belief. This may be why the bulk of psychiatrist Ian Stevenson's cases on reincarnation took place in countries where Eastern religions dominated. [13]

Stevenson, who was a professor of medicine at the University of Virginia, became internationally recognized for his research of reincarnation.

---

13   Walter Semkiw. "The Reincarnation Research of Ian Stevenson, MD of the University of Virginia Division of Perceptual Studies." *Institute for the Integration of Science, Intuition and Spirit (IISIS)*. http://www.iisis.net/index .php%3Fpage%3Dsemkiw-ian-stevenson-reincarnation-past-lives-research.

He discovered evidence suggesting memories and physical injuries could pass from one lifetime to another. He studied 2,500 children, mostly from Asia and India, who reported past-life memories soon after they were able to speak. In nearly half of the cases, Stevenson was able to find supporting evidence, including birthmarks linked to a previous lifetime. For example, if the cause of death of the previous life was a knife wound to the neck, the child might have a birthmark on the same side of the neck. Likewise, the child might have a strong dislike or fear of knives.

Cultural and religious beliefs help to explain some of the experiences Isabella Dove had after her young daughter tragically died of malaria. Isabella was one of our early blogging friends, a truly nomadic spirit, Italian by birth, who has lived in Southeast Asia for years. When we first met her, she and her daughter, Naa'ila Gioia, were living in Thailand. They moved to Laos and traveled frequently to India and west Africa, where they lived when Naa'ila died.

"My daughter passed away on October 23, 2014. She was 11 years, 9 months and 9 days old. The day she died was the Diwali Festival, or as they call it in India, the Festival of Lights. It's a day when many people apparently wish they could pass away because the Festival of Lights represents the ultimate liberation from life's burdens. It occurs every year around the end of October."

"I was told that some people in India who are on their way to the other side actually try to wait to pass away on that day. So when I was in India, people were telling me how lucky my daughter and I were that she passed on the day she did. She was freed from burden and went straight to the light and this had invaluable significance for my own karma."

Since cremations weren't permitted in west Africa at that time, Isabella decided to take her daughter's body to Europe and have a cremation there, possibly with Theravada Buddhist blessings. Her ex-husband offered to help. He contacted several temples and found a Vietnamese monk who was willing to do the ceremony. But Isabella wanted a practitioner of Theravada Buddhism, which she follows.

Her ex mailed her the next day that he'd found a monk and a temple officially authorized to conduct this type of ceremony. Both were recognized by the Belgian Ministry of Foreign Affairs and the Administration of Capital City of Brussels. "I arrived in Belgium on Tuesday, October 28, 2014, and went straight to the Wat Thai Dhammaram Temple on the outskirts of the capital city. As I walked up the stairs to the entrance, beneath a beautiful blue sky, my heart beat hard and fast. Even though I have practiced Buddhism since 1982, I felt like I was going to meet an angel. Something terrible, my daughter's death, was about to be converted into something very etheric."

When the monk entered the empty room where Isabella and her friend waited, they bowed their heads to the floor three times, a Buddhist practice when in the presence of a monk. When Isabella closed the entry door, the monk said to leave it a bit open to let a little black kitten enter the room.

The kitten's name, the monk said, was *happiness long life.* Isabella immediately felt the presence of her daughter's spirit; her second name, Gioia, meant "happiness." Naa'ila had also loved cats and two weeks before she died, had told Isabella that when she died, she wanted to return as a cat and that she was certain she'd been a cat in past lives.

"This little black kitten was really a gift. It made me chuckle yet also drew tears because it was a sign that Naa'ila was amongst us. We let him walk in and that little black ball lightly jumped to me and then went and put itself to sleep on my friend's hands, which were in meditation pose."

They chatted with the monk in broken Thai and English and conducted a brief ceremony with a picture of Naa'ila. "For a few silent moments I cried my heart out. These moments were intense. My heart was letting go of sadness, the monk's energy was lifting me up. He was repeating this sentence, which is forever cast in my heart: *She left quickly, peacefully and will return quickly and peacefully. She is on holiday.*"

They discussed a few logistical arrangements for the cremation itself which was to be held the following Thursday at the main city's crematorium at 15:15. The time itself was another synchronicity for Isabella, another bit of evidence that her daughter was with them, because 15:15 (3:15 p.m.) was the end of her school day. "No other choice of time could have been more appropriate."

The cremation started promptly at 15:15 on Thursday, October 30, 2014, with a few family members and friends. They were all wearing pink or light colors as requested. "The monk's energy was filling up the room and at some very special moment the hard, white neon light of the room turned pink. Probably only I could see this. Nevertheless, when I received some pictures taken during the ceremony, the light indeed was pink. My daughter was there, showing them the way, greeting me.

"At the very same moment, in the capital city of Burkina Faso, Ouagadougou, a peaceful, popular uprising was kicking out the long-standing president and the country became the first ever in Africa to experience a peaceful uprising to change twenty-seven years of history. Burkina Faso also happens to be the West African country where I first walked just one week after the cremation of my own father in that same crematorium were my Naa'ila was cremated."

As Isabella's experience illustrates, signs and symbols that spirits use to communicate are dependent upon culture and belief systems. In the West, cremations are usually performed in a funeral home and the unlikely appearance of a black kitten probably wouldn't be associated with the spirit of the dead. If anything, it would be seen as a dark omen, like black cats on Halloween. But for Isabella, the appearance of that cat was a sign that her daughter was present.

Upon her return to Laos from Europe, Isabella continued to have contact with Naa'ila. She organized a Theravada Buddhist ceremony at the main temple in Vientiane, the capital and largest city in Laos, where she wanted to put her daughter's ashes in the wall of the temple. To do this, she needed a plaque. "The best way for me was to keep it simple, creative, and not too expensive. So I took the picture of her that I love and on it wrote: *May all experience kindness, love, beauty, grace, life, peace, here, now, and infinite.*"

Isabella went to a print shop and had the plaque made on an acrylic support that would be covered with glass and sealed. She had two additional copies made so she could keep one and send the other to her brother in Europe. It cost her four times the price of the three acrylic plaques to mail one to Europe, which went out around January 20, 2015.

Isabella couldn't find a bubble-protected envelope, so she put the plaque in a simple envelope and figured she would be lucky if the package arrived at its destination in one piece. Even though the mail in Laos is reliable, there were no guarantees. After a month or so, her brother told her the package hadn't arrived yet.

"Then, on March 10, 2015, he was writing me a happy birthday e-mail and announced the package had arrived that very day, on my birthday. Like a present. So my lovely daughter's presence was in both places at the same time—in Europe with my brother and with me in Thailand, wishing me a happy birthday!"

Isabella continues to document her contact and communication with her daughter on her blog. She hopes that what she has experienced may help other parents who have lost children.

Sometimes, life has a way of bringing the death of a loved one full circle. It does this through a synchronicity that is so clearly a sign of spirit contact that everyone involved recognizes it as such.

Other Types of Signs

At pivotal junctures in our lives, synchronicities proliferate. They become beacons that guide, confirm, comfort, and reassure, and quite often they are precursors to spirit contact. Just ask writer Dale Dassel.

In 2014, his mother was diagnosed with lung cancer. The disease was managed for a while with radiation and chemo, but in December 2015, the cancer spread to her brain and she underwent surgery to remove a tumor. Then in early March 2016, an MRI revealed the cancer had spread to her spine. Dale and his father spent a week with her in the hospital and she was finally released into home hospice care. Doctors initially said she had a month left, but the hospice told Dale and his dad that, realistically, she had about a week.

In mid-March, Dale e-mailed us about his mother's situation. "We are trying to keep her as comfortable as possible, just as we always promised her. Mom was always practical and matter-of-fact about her cancer, and has been preparing us for it since the beginning. That's a blessing now because her words have given us strength to carry on amid our grief. She's been sedated and sleeping since her stay in the hospital, and it's just a matter of time now.

"This afternoon I was outside with our dogs while the nurse was visiting to check on Mom's condition. I was sitting on the patio when something flew into my shirt and landed on my chest. I reached into my shirt and found a ladybug crawling on my hand. I've always considered ladybugs a sign of good luck and happiness, and immediately realized it as a sign from Mom. I mentally spoke to it, promising that we would keep her as comfortable as possible until she leaves us, how much we love her, and I asked her to give us a sign when she reaches the other side. The ladybug remained perfectly still on the tip of my index finger for about ten minutes, then a gust of wind swept across the yard. It flew off into the clear blue sky, carrying my promise with it. My spirit is lifted, but it will still be devastating when she passes."

The ladybug as a sign of communication with his comatose mother comforted Dale and reassured him that her death would be peaceful. And it was.

On the one-month anniversary of his mother's death, Dale e-mailed us with an update. "Things have finally settled down. But something really amazing happened last night around 12:30 a.m. as I was reading in bed. I began to grow drowsy, so I put the novel aside and lay calmly, gazing around my room just thinking about life but nothing in particular.

"I was about to open the book to resume reading when I heard Mom's voice clearly in my mind: *I can hear you now*. It seemed to come from immediately beside me, as if she were standing right by the bed. If my eyes had been closed, I would've sworn she just opened the door and walked into the room. The words were spoken with absolute calm; a matter-of-fact statement in her own voice, crystal clear. I looked in the direction of the voice in mild surprise, as it was completely out of the blue. I wasn't even thinking about Mom, and she had never said that to me before, so I don't have a mental sound byte of that sentence. She had spoken to me."

That message, *I can hear you now*, seems to suggest that Dale's mother has rested and recovered from her long illness and is attuned to her loved ones who remain behind.

As Robert Hopcke wrote in *There Are No Accidents: Synchronicity and the Stories of Our Lives,* "At times, the synchronistic meaning of a coincidence seems almost capable of repairing and making whole what death has torn asunder." [14]

PRACTICE 3: PERSONAL SIGNS AND SYMBOLS

Even if you haven't experienced spirit communication, you undoubtedly recognize certain signs and symbols as personally significant in context with a deceased loved one. It might be something as simple as spotting your late father's lucky number on the way to work. Or perhaps a friend or your spouse gives you a bouquet of your mother's favorite

---

14   Robert Hopcke. *There Are No Accidents: Synchronicity and the Stories of Our Lives* (New York: Riverhead Books, 1997), 237.

flowers just as you were missing her. Or you see an eagle circling above your house, a bird you associate with a deceased friend. Any of these signs and symbols could be what spirits of the deceased use to initiate contact, and that you experience as meaningful coincidences.

The more personal the sign or symbol was to the deceased, the more likely that it's an example of genuine contact. For that reason, you might want to compile a related list in your journal. Think back to your experiences with your deceased loved one and see if you can recall any of these potential signs or symbols that might appear to you.

The Text Message

There are times when spirit contact is so direct and immediate you can't mistake it for anything else. Just ask Nancy Atkinson of Portland, Oregon.

In May 2016, Nancy's husband Rich was diagnosed with glioblastoma, the same type of brain cancer that Senator John McCain has and that killed Anne Strieber. He was given twelve to fifteen months to live. He died September 27, 2017.

Nancy and her daughters were having a difficult time in the aftermath of Rich's death. Every day, the hope that he would walk through the front door faded away. Then on November 18, Nancy started going through his clothes, a kind of admission that he really wasn't going to come back, and texted her daughters, Jen and Jill. The exchange went something like this, Nancy says:

Nancy to both daughters: *Are you coming today to help with Dad's clothes?*

Jen: *I guess.*

Nancy: *What time?*

Jen: *I don't know. I'm tired. When do you want me? Noon?*

Nancy: *It should only take about an hour. Noon is fine.*

Jen: *OK.*

Jill: *No, I said tomorrow.*

Nancy started to respond to Jill when the words *He loves you* typed out on the line.

Nancy was so shocked that it took her a moment to continue.

Nancy: *I didn't type that! It was right in the middle of the thread and I did not type it!*

Jen: *What?!*

Nancy: *That just popped up on my thread!! I didn't type that!!*

Jen: *Weird!*

Nancy: *OMG*

Jen: *He loves us!*

What's particularly interesting about this contact is that when Rich was alive, he was a big texter. "I could be upstairs, he could be downstairs, and he would text me. This happened while I was texting with my daughters, not during any other conversation," Nancy wrote us. "It made my day."

Practice 4: Identifying Signs and Symbols
His/her:

Favorite numbers _____

Favorite colors _____

Favorite books _____

Favorite movies _____

Favorite animals _____

Favorite birds _____

Your Methods

If you have experienced spirit communication, which methods work best for you to initiate contact? Check the ones that apply to you.

- Meditation

- Dream incubation

- Channeled writing

- Summoning through intense desire

- Remaining aware

- Making a request

- Setting an intention

- Other

Keep this list handy. You'll be adding to it! If you haven't yet experienced spirit communication, don't worry. We'll get more into the details of these practices in the chapters ahead.

3

❋

White Feathers
& Other Objects

IT SEEMS SOMEWHAT ironic that objects, the physical things that link us to our everyday world, are also tools that spirits use to signal us of their presence. The object might be a clock, a radio, a book, a lamp, or an item from the natural world, such as a white feather, as in the following example.

Over a period of sixteen months, Mike Perry of the UK lost three loved ones—his daughter, his mother, and his closest friend of thirty years. After his mother's death, he began seeing white feathers everywhere. On one occasion, shortly after his friend had died, he was walking across the square in his town, wondering if his friend was okay. Out of nowhere, a white feather appeared and dropped at his feet.

As he continued to walk, the feather was swept up in a gust of wind, flew ahead of him, then did a big forward circle before falling again at his feet. On another occasion, after the death of his daughter, Mike and his wife were out walking and came across a white feather where no feathers should have been. His wife picked it up and said, "Look, she's thinking of us."

White feathers, for many who have lost loved ones, are a sign from the other side that the deceased is alive and well in the spirit world.

An Angel Watching Over Her

One day, Gloria was hurrying to her car, late for a meeting, when she found a white feather resting on the driveway near the driver's side. She picked it up, recognizing it as a message from her daughter telling her to slow down. She picked it up, smiled, and said, "Hi, Caron," then tucked the feather in her blouse, close to her heart. Caron Keating, who had been a popular TV and radio host in the UK, died in 2004, at age forty-one, of breast cancer. She left behind two young sons.

Gloria is convinced Caron has been her guardian angel for the past decade. "People may think I am deluded, but I know she is there for me, protecting and comforting me whenever I need her most," she said in an article she wrote for the *Daily Mail* newspaper on September 26, 2014, with the lengthy headline: 'White feathers that convince Gloria Hunniford guardian angels DO exist … and make her certain that her darling daughter Caron Keating is watching over her.' [15]

Gloria remembers Caron telling her long before her illness that a single white feather was an angel's calling card. The first time she found a white feather was nine months after Caron's death. "We were on our way to Disneyland Paris with Caron's two sons, who were ten and seven. It was meant to be a birthday treat for the seven-year-old, but trudging along the rain-soaked platform at Folkestone, Kent, hand-in-hand with the boys, I felt consumed with memories. It wasn't just the lashing rain that dampened my mood."

---

15   Gloria Hunniford. "White feathers that convince Gloria Hunniford guardian angels DO exist … and make her certain that her darling daughter Caron Keating is watching over her." *Daily Mail, Sept. 26, 2014.* http://www.dailymail.co.uk/news/article-2771542/White-feathers-convince-Gloria-Hunniford-guardian-angels-DO-exist-make-certain-darling-daughter-Caron-Keating-watching-her.html.

She went on to say that she was feeling pain and despair. "For the boys' sake, I was trying to put on a brave face. But inside I was breaking apart. Then suddenly I looked down and there on my shoe was a single, snow-white feather. It had quite literally dropped from the sky. There was no rational explanation. Caron's words from long before she died came flooding back to me: 'Remember Mum. If an isolated white feather appears out of nowhere, it's a sign that your guardian angel is watching over you.'"

Caron talked with her mother on several occasions about angels and even made a documentary about them. It was as if she was preparing for a future role on the other side.

In September 2016, we did an Internet search using the term *white feathers as messages from the deceased* and more than 95,000 links appeared. Two months later, in mid-November 2016, we searched the term again and *275,000* links appeared. In January 2018, a Google search for the same words yielded 688,000 links. This uptick of links may suggest the phenomenon is growing or that more people are becoming aware of it.

White feathers are one of the most common ways our deceased loved ones are thought to communicate with us. Since it cuts across cultures and spiritual traditions, it could well be an archetype of spirit communication.

Objects that are directly linked to a deceased person can be even more startling. After Rob's father died, his mother Ione found the initials *MAC* inscribed in the frost on a window. It was next to the chair where her late husband had spent most of his days reading in his latter years. Mac was his nickname.

Shooting Stars

On July 5, 2014, Risa's husband Ron proposed to her beneath a sky filled with shooting stars. "What was interesting is that after Ron proposed, we saw shooting stars that entire summer. I have never seen more shooting stars in my entire life," wrote Risa, a high school history teacher in South Carolina.

For more than a year, she didn't see another shooting star. Then, on November 2, 2015, Risa's father, who had been best man at her wedding, passed away. "The night he died, Ron and I saw a shooting star, and it was no ordinary shooting star. It was around 4 a.m. in Greenville and we were driving home from mom and dad's, where he had died. A shooting star literally careened out of the sky and looked as if it might hit the front end of our car."

It was so startling that Ron pulled over to the side of the road. "It was the weirdest thing, but I swear it just shot right for the car. And though it didn't actually hit us, it sure looked like it was going to. Daddy was a massive practical joker and startling people was his favorite thing to do, so we figured he got us again! It was incredible because we both instantly knew it was Dad. As soon as we pulled over, we looked at each other and both of us said, 'Pops!' You could feel it in your bones that it was Dad letting us know he was okay."

Incubating Contact through Objects

We met Risa when she mentioned in one of her Facebook posts that one of our books on synchronicity seriously changed her life. We were curious about what she meant so Trish asked her how the book affected her. Risa's explanation provides a good example of the mindset that serves as a means of incubating contact by making connections you wouldn't normally see.

"It has allowed me to find synchronicity in everything I experience. The concept and explanation has been vital in the loss of my dad. I watch for meaning in events that may seem unrelated at first, but lead to something profound."

When you increase your awareness of synchronicity and can link the appearance of certain objects to lost loved ones, you open the possibility of more direct contact. For example, after Risa made the connection of the shooting star to her deceased father, he seemed to reward her with a personal appearance. "I was washing dishes when I looked up and, out of the corner of my eye, I glimpsed a man behind me, wearing a white t-shirt. I dropped the dish I was holding and started to shake. I knew it wasn't a reflection. The TV was off and my curtains were closed. When I swung around, no one was there. But the thought came to mind that when my dad died, he was wearing a white t-shirt. I know it was him. He was letting me know he was still around. I started crying, but at the same time his appearance brought me much comfort."

Many Means of Contact

There are a variety of ways spirits might make contact related to objects. Some of the most common include the following:

- Objects mysteriously disappear and reappear in other locations.

- A clock stops working at the time of death of a loved one. Alternately, a clock starts working at the time related to the deceased person's life. Or the timing is related to an event of importance to the spirit, such as a death, birth, marriage, or divorce.

- A reflection in a mirror or window of a face that isn't physically present.

- Lights, a TV, a radio, or other electronic devices come on when talking about a lost loved one.

- An object of significance to the deceased, such as a book or a figurine, inexplicably falls from a shelf.

- Objects appear where they don't belong and seem to address a question about someone who has passed on.

- The repeated appearance of a type of bird or other animal that is rarely seen.

- Unexpectedly finding an object that belonged to or was important to a deceased loved one.

- Initials or names appearing on steamed or frosted glass windows.

Practice 5: Contact through Objects

Have you experienced spirit contact through an object? If so, what object or objects came into play? In your journal, write about your experiences related to objects linked to contact. If you've had a number of such experiences, was it always the same object or were different objects used? Have you noticed a pattern?

A Meaningful Charm

Marie was diagnosed with lung cancer about two years ago. She was feeling scared and lonely, so she asked her parents—who were both deceased—for a sign that everything would be okay. Several weeks later she was walking across the rug in her living room and stepped on something sharp. She looked in the rug and found a little silver faith, hope, and charity charm her parents had given her years ago.

She couldn't figure out how the charm had gotten into the rug since she'd last seen it in a box within another box in her underwear drawer. She asked her partner, Terry, if he'd taken the charm out, but he didn't know what she was talking about, and she hadn't told him about her request for a sign from her parents. She took it as a sign from her parents to have hope and faith. She felt reassured.

Marie's experience was meaningful to her as an example of spirit contact through an object. She had set her intention on contacting her deceased parents. She was feeling upset about her condition and put a lot of emotion behind her intentions. Then she made her request, sent it out into the cosmos, and released it.

It took several weeks before she came upon the charm mysteriously hidden in the rug. Perhaps the charm had been there for weeks, waiting to be found. Regardless, she received her answer in the words on the charm—faith, hope, and charity. Also, think about the word *charm*, which has more than one meaning. Besides being a small ornament worn on a necklace or bracelet, it also means something achieved by magic, and also the power to delight and cause admiration. It all fits!

Electronics

Electronics are one of the favored methods spirits use for contact. Even in the days before cell phones and the Internet, spirits used radios, landlines, and recording devices for communication. The electronic voice phenomenon—EVP—is sounds on electronic recordings that may be the voices of spirits unintentionally recorded or that have been requested to communicate. Professional ghost hunters use digital voice recorders for EVP as well as a host of other gadgets. The equipment ranges from EVP recorders to meters that measure electromagnetic frequency, infrared and thermal cameras, motion sensors, and full-spectrum video cameras. On ghoststop.com, one of the most popular gadgets is called a Spirit Box.

Spirit Boxes use radio frequency sweeps, both AM and FM, to generate white noise that supposedly provides entities the energy they need to communicate. Sometimes voices or sounds can be heard above the static, according to ghoststop.com. Ghost hunters contend such sounds are attempts to communicate and sometimes familiar names can be heard.

On May 26, 2011, Kira lost her oldest son, Tom, in a car accident. In the aftermath, Kira saved Tom's cell phone and to her surprise, it became a link to him. "My son's cell phone battery remained charged for two years after his death. I would turn it on occasionally just to see his photos and to hear a voice recording. Then I would turn it off after listening. I have never heard of a phone staying charged that long without it being recharged."

Around the two-year anniversary of his death, the phone battery finally died. "But I would like to think that he had a little something to do with it staying charged for so long. The first two years after a child dies is said to be the most difficult and is considered 'new grief' and the phone stayed charged for the most difficult years."

On Friday, April 1, 2016, Kira's two grown sons surprised her by stopping by. "They are rarely home at the same time and I was very happy about it. So I posted on Facebook *All my guys are home tonight! What a pleasant surprise.*"

What occurred next left her speechless. "Out of nowhere, a Word document popped up on my computer screen, covering my Facebook page. I was shocked when I saw the title: *Dreaming of My Son.*" It was a poem she'd written about a dream she'd had several years earlier. In the dream, she and Tom were walking hand in hand. "It's one of my most prized visitation dreams I've ever experienced."

Kira said she'd been thinking a lot about Tom, and the synchronicity left her with a feeling that he was here with her, along with her other sons.

Three days later, Kira visited a friend and before she said anything about her recent experiences, her friend said it was a time for synchronicities and that she should be open and aware of them. "When I got home I started to connect it all together. Wow, is all I could say."

PRACTICE 6: CRYSTAL CAVE MEDITATION

This meditation is particularly effective for manifesting spirit contact related to objects. Perhaps the method works because the meditation ultimately focuses on visualized objects.

Begin by moving into a relaxed state of mind at a place and time when you won't be interrupted. Focus on your breath as you take several deep inhalations and relaxing exhalations. Then shift your focus inward and scan your body. Concentrate on how your various body parts feel, starting with your feet, ankles, lower legs, knees, thighs, hips and belly, back, chest, shoulders, neck, and internal organs. Take your time. Feel your body relaxing. Remain focused and concentrate. Nothing else matters.

Now turn your concentration to your bodily functions. Maybe you become aware of the beat of your heart and the flow of blood from your heart, arteries, capillaries, and veins taking it back to your heart. If you can't hear the beat of your heart, imagine you can. You might go deeper into the self—beyond the physical and into interior landscapes—the invisible nonphysical part of your being, which is really your true self. Stay with it. Gentle breathing. Concentrating. Relaxing.

Next, imagine you're following a path through a verdant forest. You feel the crackle of leaves and brittle twigs under your feet, and smell the fertile scent of growing things. You feel the warmth of the day. Gradually, you reach flagstone steps and slowly climb a slope until you reach a heavy wooden door with a rounded top. It opens into a shadowy tunnel, but you can see light in the distance. You step inside and follow the tunnel until you reach a massive cavern filled with enormous crystals. You see luminous, glimmering crystal everywhere, on the walls, ceiling, and floor. You feel a high energy streaming through you as you sense you've entered a sacred place. Know that this chamber magnifies your ability to make contact with the other side. You are also aware you will be safe and protected, and whatever contact is made will be comforting and elevating.

Think of a deceased loved one, a family member, relative, or friend that you want to contact. Or maybe you're seeking communion with a spirit guide. You see a mirror like no other among all the glittering crystals. The surface shimmers and swirls and you move closer. Take your time as you stare intently into the mirror.

Gradually, an image forms and it's the one you are seeking. You feel warmth and happiness emanating from this spirit being. You might hear a message and maybe you start a dialogue. Ask the spirit to make contact with you again in your everyday life through an object that will prove to you the contact is real. Take your time; stay focused.

Finally, thank your loved one or spirit guide, and watch the being fade away into the mirror. Now feel yourself lifting up with the energy and leaving the crystal cavern through the roof. Go with the flow. Become aligned with the energy, moving with it. And you're back where you began.

Our loved ones who have passed on use anything they can to communicate with us—cell phones, feathers and other objects, number clusters, and even two-year-old Word documents. But how does that work, what mechanism, what operating system allows spirits to manipulate matter and the objects they are getting our attention with? Here are three possible theories.

1. Spirit Psychokinesis

Psychokinesis is the ability to affect objects with our minds. When the inexplicable movement of objects is linked to after-death communication, then in theory we're dealing with effects created by the consciousness of the deceased. Skeptics might quickly dismiss such events as wishful thinking or misinterpretation of the evidence. However, when such events happen to you, they are jarring and grab your attention.

Spirit psychokinesis isn't limited to knocking sounds, voices, or electronics or electrical devices that turn off and on by themselves. The phenomenon manifests in numerous ways—initials or names inscribed on steamy or frosty glass; objects that fall off shelves; glass that shatters for no reason; objects found where they shouldn't be or that disappear and reappear. The challenge, of course, is to determine which such incidents have normal explanations and which ones are examples of contact with the other side.

When the apparent movement of objects without physical cause is dramatic, startling, and even frightening, such incidents are typically referred to as *poltergeist phenomenon.* Many investigators relate such incidents to the power of the unconscious mind. In particular, researchers notice in many cases an adolescent child, often female, was nearby.

One such investigator was Carl Jung, who, while a university student, took an interest in a young female cousin who, near the age of puberty, would go into a trance and speak in strange voices, as if possessed. During the time of these experiences, the family dinner table split apart with a loud cracking sound, he explained in his biography, *Memories, Dreams, Reflections.* "The table top had split from the rim to beyond the center, and not along any joint; the split ran through solid wood." [16]

Another time an explosion was heard from a sideboard and Jung found a bread knife had shattered in several pieces. But Jung didn't relate the powerful blasts to the presence of any spirits. He called these events *exteriorization phenomenon,* and thought the incidents were related to the presence of his disturbed cousin.

Possibly both explanations are true. The unconscious power of an adolescent or others could energize a spirit, giving it the ability to manipulate matter. Then one might ask: Is it the spirit that is angry or upset, or is it the human who has empowered the spirit?

2. As Above, So Below

The concept in this theory is that physical reality is a temporary extension of our true reality in the spirit realm. Spirits not only can nudge objects and impact physical reality in a variety of ways, they can also manifest as humans, and they do so with the birth of *every* child. In other words, they are *us* and our essential reality is the spirit realm. While it's surprising when these nudges from the spirit world occur, in essence

---

16   C.G. Jung. *Memories, Dreams, Reflections.* (New York: Vintage, reissue edition, 1989), 105.

the spirit world is not so divorced from our reality as we may think. While it seems we are physical beings seeking spiritual experiences, in truth we are all spiritual beings experiencing physical existences.

Emanuel Swedenborg, the renowned eighteenth-century Swedish scientist, philosopher, and mystic, supported such ideas about the nature of reality. He contended in *Journal of Dreams and Spiritual Experiences: In the Year Seventeen Hundred and Forty-Four* [17] that the afterlife was the primary reality and that physical reality flowed from it. In other words, the physical reality unfolds from the inner reality.

More than two centuries later, physicist David Bohm proposed a similar theory in his book, *Wholeness and the Implicate Order*. [18] According to Bohm, the implicate or enfolded order is the deeper reality, a primal soup that births everything in the universe, even space and time. He referred to our external reality as the explicate order. Perhaps synchronicity and other aspects of the paranormal exist along the border between the two and this border is our most accessible access to the enfolded order.

Interestingly, these ideas echo the accumulated research on near-death experiences and beliefs in most shamanic traditions, where excursions into the afterlife through trance and out-of-body travel are frequent occurrences.

3. Greater Consciousness and Our Interconnection

A clock stops at the exact minute of a loved one's death. A broken radio, owned by the deceased, begins to play when you're talking about the person. You open a book and find the picture of your lost loved one just as you were talking about an event from his or her life. These examples of spirit contact are also synchronicities that come into play related to

---

17   Emanuel Swedenborg. *Emanuel Swedenborg's Journal of Dreams and Spiritual Experiences: In the Year Seventeen Hundred and Forty-Four (Classic Reprint).* (London: Forgotten Books, 2017.)

18   David Bohm. *Wholeness and the Implicate Order.* (London: Routledge, 2002.)

spirit communication through objects. Such events occur outside of cause and effect and are meaningful to the observer.

Such events seem to indicate nudges from the other side, a momentary blending of a deeper reality with our everyday reality—the implicate touching the explicate. In other words, spirit contact as synchronicity reveals the reality of a greater consciousness in which everyone and everything alive and in spirit are interconnected. Physicist Victor Mansfield wrote in *Synchronicity, Science, and Soulmaking,* that we live in "a radically interconnected and interdependent world, one so essentially connected at a deep level that the interconnections are more fundamental, more real than the independent existence of the parts." [19]

These ideas are echoed in Eastern spiritual traditions. The *Rigveda,* an ancient Indian text, echoes these ideas. Indra, the king of gods and god of war, casts a massive spiritual net (now known as Indra's Net) in which all beings are interconnected. So a single tug ripples across the entire net.

The Hindu term *Brahman* refers to the fundamental connection of all things in the universe. The appearance of this universal oneness in the soul is called *Atman.* Zen Buddhism refers to *satori,* a sense of unity felt with the universe and an awareness of the compassionate intelligence that permeates the most minute details. *Chi,* according to Chinese philosophy, is the life force that permeates all things and empowers the universe.

These Eastern philosophies are similar to the concept of the noosphere, a notion created by Pierre Teilhard de Chardin, a French philosopher, paleontologist, and ordained Jesuit priest who was prominent in the first half of the twentieth century. [20] He was convinced of the existence of an invisible "ordering intelligence," a mental sphere that links all humanity. He proposed that as mankind organizes itself in

---

19   Victor Mansfield. *Synchronicity, Science, and Soulmaking: Understanding Jungian Synchronicity Through Physics, Buddhism, and Philosophy.* (Chicago: Open Court Books, 1998), 226.

20   Pierre Teilhard De Chardin. *Pierre Teilhard De Chardin: Writings.* (Maryknoll, NY: Orbis Books, 1999), 55.

more complex social networks, the noosphere expands in awareness. Considering the vast expansion of the social media on the Internet, it seems this noosphere of interconnectedness would be experiencing rapid growth in the twenty-first century. Yet, on the level of the everyday world of politics, it seems as if the opposite is true. On the surface, that appears the case. However, at a deeper level of awareness, we're all interconnected with the diversity of viewpoints, even those we find appalling in our everyday lives.

Objects from the Past

Historically, glass, mirrors, or other reflective material—water, stones, crystal balls—have been favored objects for spirit communication, and been a part of some esoteric traditions.

In the sixteenth century, Queen Elizabeth was intrigued with an Aztec mirror owned by John Dee, an English mathematician, astronomer, and astrologer. Made of highly polished obsidian, the mirror was used as a vehicle of spirit communication. It was said that visions would appear by gazing into it while in a receptive state of mind. The Queen believed she saw the spirit of a dead friend while gazing into the Aztec mirror.

The ancient Greeks not only believed the dead could communicate with the living, but the living could contact the dead. They built underground chambers known as *psychomanteums*, where priests organized encounters between the living and dead. The ruins of one exist near the River Acherton.

Dr. Raymond Moody, best known for his classic book on near-death experiences, *Life After Life*, became fascinated by the concept of the psychomanteums. He saw them as a way of making contact with the dead without having to die briefly and be revived. Moody, a scholar of ancient Greece, read the Greek magical papyri—scrolls of magical recipes found in Egypt, but written in Greek. "By following the instruction of the magical papyri in a facility designed for just this purpose, I had created a modern psychomanteum in the style of the ancient Greeks," he wrote in his autobiography, *Paranormal: My Life in Pursuit of the Afterlife.*[21]

Moody called it the John Dee Memorial Theater of the Mind, and began looking for people willing to step into his apparition booth. His goal was to answer this question: Can apparitions of deceased loved ones make themselves known in a controlled environment to normal, healthy people?

In preparation, he spent hours with his patients discussing the loved one they wanted to encounter. Then he escorted the patient into his mirror-gazing booth and turned on a light about as bright as a single candle. He instructed the patient to relax, gaze deeply into the mirror, and think only of the one she wanted to see. There was no time limit. After the person finally emerged from the booth, she discussed her experiences with Moody.

Moody was surprised that five of his first ten subjects saw and communicated with an apparition, and all five believed that they had actually connected with a deceased loved one. He had expected one or two would make contact and then doubt that it was a true encounter.

His first subject, a forty-four-year-old nurse whose husband had died two years earlier, made contact, but not in the way she or Moody expected. They talked for hours about her late husband, but when she emerged from the booth, she had a puzzled expression. She had made contact, but with her father, not her husband. She was stunned by the experience, because he actually come out of the mirror to talk to her.

PRACTICE 7: SCRYING FOR CONTACT
Do you ever stare at clouds and see images? That's a simplistic example of scrying, a form of divination. Scrying typically makes use of a mirror, crystals, a bowl of water, or any other reflective surface to divine the future

---

21   Raymond Moody and Paul Perry. *Paranormal: My Life in Pursuit of the Afterlife.* (New York: HarperOne, 2013), 188.

or connect with the spirit world. If you'd like to try your hand at scrying to initiate spirit contact, here are some tips to do so safely and effectively:

- The best tool for you is the one that works. A bowl of water might serve your purpose better than a $500 dollar crystal ball. A hand mirror or a shiny piece of black obsidian can also work as a focal point to help you bridge the spirit and physical worlds. You're looking for images or symbols you wouldn't ordinarily notice.

- Don't approach scrying in a frivolous manner. It's not a form of entertainment or a party trick. Maintain a joyful, expectant attitude and remain open to the possibility of contact. If you're certain it's not possible, then your experience probably will reflect that belief.

- Before you begin, surround yourself with protective energy. Maybe you visualize your entire body surrounded by white or gold light. You can also call upon spirit guides or angels to block out negative entities and only allow positive spirits to come into your field of energy.

- Choose a time and place with few, if any, distractions. Turn off your cell phone. Enter a relaxed, meditative state of mind. Light candles and incense and play tranquil music. Dim the lights.

- Know your intention. Feel your desire, and state your request. If you're more comfortable initially trying to see future events rather than attempting to make contact with the deceased, then start there. Eventually you can work your way into spirit communication. At the beginning, the point is to be at ease with whatever tool you're using.

- Take a few slow, deep breaths, relaxing deeper with each exhalation. When you're fully relaxed and centered, repeat your request and focus on the object of your choice—water, crystal, a mirror. Take your time. Remain relaxed and let your gaze go soft. You might pose a question now related to your request.

- Have a pen and paper handy. When you scry, you're entering an altered state, just as you do when you dream. Your impressions are fleeting, quickly forgotten. Record any images, symbols, or words you heard as soon as you finish. If you don't get results the first time, keep trying. The more you practice, the easier it is to get into a meditative state and pick up sensory responses, even subtle ones. Consider keeping a scrying journal similar to a dream journal to record your impressions.

- Pay attention to synchronicities that occur before, during, and after scrying. The synchronicities are apt to be powerful, their messages direct, unambiguous. Record them immediately.

- Spirit contact through scrying sometimes provides glimpses into the future. Rather than trying to interpret what you're seeing as you're seeing it, just record your impressions as you would when you awaken from a dream. Then be alert for occurrences, people, names, and clusters of synchronicities that are similar to what you experienced when you scried.

Message in the Air Vent

In the months following the death of Leah's grandfather, she experienced several points of contact with him. A few months after he died, Leah sat on the back porch of her grandparents' farmhouse, where she lived and took care of her grandmother.

"It was two or three a.m. and just as hot and still as could be. As I was sitting there, a cylindrical air vent on top of the garage started spinning very slowly in a clockwise direction. It was one of two air vents that my grandfather and I had installed many years ago. There was absolutely no breeze and it was so hot and humid it was air you could wear.

"What really floored me was that only one of the vents was spinning. The other didn't move at all. I got goose bumps and said, 'Grandpa, if you are making this vent spin would you please give me a sign?'"

She waited a few moments to see what would happen. The vent completely stopped, then very slowly started spinning again. "Knowing he was there, I must have talked to him for at least ten minutes, and the entire time the vent moved at a snail's pace. Then, just as suddenly as it began, it stopped. I was so gobsmacked. I just sat there and cried and thanked him for coming to see me."

4

❁

Sounds, Scents
& Sensations

WHEN YOU THINK of spirit contact, what comes immediately to mind? For many of us, the answer is a visual image of the lost loved one or friend. Even if it's a fleeting one or a ball of light rather than an ethereal body, seeing is believing. But that's not the way it always works. It could be that some spirits don't have the ability to manifest a visual image. Or possibly the blame lies with us. Maybe they are right here with us and we can't see them for whatever reason. Perhaps that's why spirits resort to other methods of contact, including sounds and scents, the topic of this chapter. The bottom line: spirits communicate with the living in whatever method that works.

Sounds

During a trip to the Dominican Republic, we stayed in a hotel on the beach of Puerto Plata, one of the best windsurfing spots in the world. The hotel consisted of three buildings forming three sides of a square with a garden in the middle. When we arrived, we found the so-called garden was actually a fenced-in graveyard. So the second-floor porch of our apartment looked out onto the nearby graveyard and the ocean beyond it.

Our daughter was freaked out by the proximity of the graveyard, so we asked if we could change apartments. The management was happy to accommodate. We moved into another building to one side of the graveyard. Now our porch looked directly to the ocean. However, our door was actually closer to the graveyard. But we decided to stay put.

We assumed it was a historical graveyard. But one day, the gate was open so we walked in. We'd barely gone ten feet when we noticed a grave marker indicating a man had been buried four months earlier. He apparently had been a windsurfer, because his gravestone was the top half of a windsurfing board, and his epitaph read: *Wherever the wind blows I will be there.*

While puzzling over this grave, which was only about thirty feet from our apartment, an old man with a shovel approached us. He was digging a grave and was excited because he'd come upon a coffin from an earlier graveyard below this one. He said the sand kept rising so graves were piled one on top of the other. He wanted to show us the grave, but we'd seen enough. As we were about to leave, Rob picked up a smooth stone from the graveyard and took it with him.

On our last night in the apartment, we fell asleep fairly early. We were both awakened around 11:30 p.m. by what sounded like a wrecking ball slamming into the walls of our suite. BAM. BAM. BAM. Then a pause. Then three more BAMs. Another pause. On the last of the next three BAMs, we sat up simultaneously.

The noise stopped. It hadn't been frightening or threatening. In fact, it had left us feeling enervated and empowered. We had made contact with the other side. Then we heard voices in the living room and found the television on, even though it was off when we went to bed. Our daughter was still asleep in the back bedroom and hadn't heard any of it.

Nothing else happened for the rest of the night. We speculated that the stone Rob had taken from the graveyard might have a spirit attached to it, perhaps that of the young windsurfer. So the next morning, Rob returned the stone to the spot where he'd found it, next to the windsurfer's grave.

As we checked out, Trish asked the clerk if there had been an earthquake during the night. "No, not that I know about," he replied. Trish told him about the nine BAMs and asked if the grounds were haunted. He laughed a bit sheepishly. "Si, si, but our ghosts are *simpatico ... friendly."*

In retrospect, we realized this was contact with a spirit who was a total stranger. What better way to seize the attention of the living than through a series of sounds so loud they woke us up.

A Town of Mediums

Cassadaga, Florida, is a Spiritualist community just north of Disney World. Established in 1894, it's now a flourishing little town where nearly every resident is a medium or psychic who specializes in spirit contact. Its sister community is Lily Dale in Cassadaga, New York. But Lily Dale is closed during the winter and Cassadaga is open year-round.

On weekends, the place is jammed with cars and tourists, all of them walking through the old, narrow streets, past Spirit Lake, in search of exactly the right medium. In search of messages from the dead! The town, in fact, was founded by medium George Colby, who, in the late 1800s, was directed by his spirit guide, Seneca, to establish a Spiritualist camp in the wilds of Florida. So Colby headed out to Florida from his home in upstate New York.

Back then, Florida was a swamp, a mosquito haven, a place of sweltering heat and wilderness so extreme that unless you had some landmarks, you would count yourself among the lost and missing. But Seneca had given Colby some landmarks—seven hills, and a lake. And in 1875, Colby arrived and five years later, he filed for a homestead of nearly seventy-five acres.

Today, Cassadaga is divided into two distinct areas and the dividing line is Cassadaga Road. Everything south of the road and behind the Cassadaga Hotel is the Spiritualist camp. For more than a century, the "real" mediums have lived in the camp. They are tested by the association for their mediumship skills, their ability to communicate with the dead. Psychics and mediums who practice on the other side of the road aren't approved by the Spiritualist Association. We've had readings with mediums both inside and outside of the camp and have found that the artificial border doesn't mean much in terms of mediumistic skills.

The camp consists of fifty-seven acres with fifty-five homes, two lakes (Colby Lake and Spirit Lake), a bookstore, gift shops, mediums, and healers. And oh yes, it has a haunted hotel.

The Cassadaga Hotel, in fact, is the hub of everything. Even though it's not officially part of the camp, it's the only place in town to stay. It was built in 1927 and although it has been renovated over the years and ownership has changed, its colorful history is a magnetic draw. On weekends during tourist season, the hotel is usually booked solid. It now features an excellent restaurant, free Wi-Fi, and it's not uncommon to see guests sitting around on the wide side porch throughout the day, exchanging stories about their readings with various mediums.

When our daughter, Megan, was a baby, the hotel wasn't quite what it is today. We went there for readings and stayed at the hotel. We were surprised that we were the only guests and later learned it was bike week in Daytona, so that was where the tourists had gone. We had our choice of rooms and selected one on the second floor, room 38. It was actually two connecting rooms that overlooked the Colby Center—now a bookstore and gift shop.

We walked around town that afternoon, pushing Megan in her stroller, and had readings with a medium we'd met several years earlier. After dinner with her in nearby Lake Helen, we returned to the hotel. We were struck by how eerily quiet it was. The hotel doesn't have an elevator, so we folded up Megan's stroller and headed up the stairs to the second floor. It was so still, the groan and creak of the steps and the old wooden floors sounded abnormally loud.

We settled in for the evening with our books. We didn't bother locking the doors because, after all, the town was deserted and the hotel was empty. What was the point? Around eleven or twelve, we turned off the lights. It was unusually chilly that night and Trish got up to scour the closet for additional blankets, found one, and fell back into bed. Just as we drifted off to sleep, we heard footfalls on the stairs. Loud footfalls. It sounded like a troop of bikers from Daytona had arrived wearing heavy boots, and one was headed our way.

Trish was spooked and whispered, "Hey, Rob, aren't we alone in the hotel?"

"That's what the guy at the desk said. Maybe he's doing his midnight rounds or something."

We lay there, listening. The footfalls became echoing thuds. It began to freak us out. The clerk, we recalled, was a short, skinny guy; these thuds sounded like a three hundred-pound monster. Trish got up and hurried into the adjoining room to get Megan. Rob turned on the lamp, but the light didn't do much to mitigate our mounting fear and panic. The thuds now sounded like something out of *The Shining*, so hard and loud it felt like the hotel was shaking. Trish put Megan on the bed and hurried over to Rob, who had his hand on the doorknob.

The heavy-footed being—human or not, live or dead—stopped right in front of our door. A sense of profound malevolence electrified the air, and for moments, neither of us moved.

"What the hell *is* it?" Trish hissed.

Rob took his hand away, and we immediately pushed a heavy wooden dresser in front of one door. When the knob turned and rattled, we simultaneously turned and snatched Megan from the bed where she slept. No telling where we thought we would escape if whatever was on the other side of that door broke in. Seconds later, the footfalls moved away from our door and down the hall and that was it. No more thudding footfalls, just silence and a sense of relief. It was over.

In retrospect, we've wondered how the dresser pushed in front of the door would stop a spirit, malevolent or otherwise. Can't ghosts drift through walls and doors as if they weren't there? But at the time, we simply acted. And maybe the very act of blocking the door—rather than the dresser itself—was enough to keep the spook out.

Or perhaps its intention wasn't to enter the room, but just to scare us. *You came here to talk to spirits, right? Well, here I am. Talk to me.*

We didn't sleep much after that. The next morning when we checked out, we asked the clerk if the hotel was haunted. He grinned awkwardly. "Oh sure. But we've only got friendly ghosts here." It even says that on the hotel website.

This experience, unlike the one in the Dominican Republic, was frightening. We felt threatened; the malevolence in the air was palpable. Why was this experience so different? We don't know, but perhaps it had something to do with the spirits involved.

As one medium said, "Spirits are as different as we, the living, are. Not all of them have our best interests at heart."

Carl Jung came to this realization as well.

During the winter of 1924, he spent vast stretches of time alone in the tower of the home he built on the shores of Lake Zurich in Bollingen, Switzerland. As author Deirdre Bair recounted in *Jung: A Biography*, he experienced "ghostly presences" in the tower. "He heard music, as if an orchestra were playing; he envisioned a host of young peasant men who seemed to be encircling the tower with much laughter, singing, and roughhousing." [22] Bair says these experiences happened only once to Jung in Bollingen, but that he never forgot them.

---

22   Deirdre Bair. *Jung: A Biography.* (New York: Little, Brown Company, 2003), 330.

When Spirit Distracts Us with Sound

When spirit contact occurs through loud, sudden sounds, it's often at the exact moment when we need to be startled out of whatever we're doing, thinking, or feeling. It's as if the spirit is determined to distract us. This is what happened to Diane, shortly after her father passed away.

She was going through some of his belongings he'd left behind at her home when he was living with her and her family: old photos, a briefcase, some of his clothes. She became very emotional and started crying. Suddenly, something crashed in the bedroom that had been his when he lived with her and her family, and she ran into the room to find out what happened.

A framed collage of family photos that had been hanging on the wall had slipped off the hook and fallen to the floor. The glass on the front had broken and the photos had slid out. The picture on top was of her dad. She immediately felt he was waving his arms at her and shouting, *Hey! I'm here. Now release your grief and move on.*

What's particularly interesting about this incident is that the framed collage had never slipped off the wall before. It was securely fastened to a bolt embedded in the wall. So how had her dad managed to loosen it and then knock it to the floor? How can a spirit manipulate physical matter? How had the spirit with whom we had contact in the Cassadaga Hotel managed to make such loud, reverberating sounds? The answer to this riddle depends on your particular belief system.

Among traditionally religious individuals, the ability of spirits to communicate with the living is usually deemed a miracle. In other words, God intervenes and enables the communication to occur.

Spiritualists believe that after death, spirits continue to evolve and part of that evolution entails helping the living in any way they can. This help entails communication, materializations and manifestations, and other tangible proof that the soul survives death. The more evolved the soul on the other side is, the more likely it is that the spirit will be successful in communicating and will do so often through a medium.

Mystics and spiritual teachers often ascribe such communications to "vibrational frequencies." When you're in the vibrational flow, they say, help and guidance are always available from nonphysical beings. Mystics refer to a veil that exists between the living and the dead and when that veil thins, contact between the living and the dead is much easier.

But the bottom line is that we, the living, don't really know how spirits are able to impact things in the physical world. Yet incidents happen and synchronicity is usually the component that tips us off and prompts us to pay attention. And these synchronicities often seem to defy the odds.

Contact at Death

If you've only had one contact with a spirit, chances are it happened near the moment of death. It's a time when spirits are likely to make their departure known, and these incidents of contact can be startling. Sometimes, a spirit will reach out to more distant relatives rather than those who are close and might be grieving and too emotional for contact.

Years ago when Jane Clifford's partner George was still alive and her daughter was just an infant, she awakened suddenly one morning, around four a.m., to hear a woman say, "Don't be afraid, dear. I've come to see the child before I go." She could see someone standing in the doorway, and Jane recognized her as Aunt Gwen, George's great-aunt.

"I was terrified. She lived in another county, two hundred miles away. I had met her only once." Aunt Gwen bent over to look at Jane's infant daughter, sleeping next to her, and then vanished.

The next morning, Jane told her partner what happened. "I think your Aunt Gwen died around four a.m., about the time she visited."

Sure enough, a relative called during breakfast to tell them Aunt Gwen had died suddenly and unexpectedly around four a.m. For Jane, the contact was auditory as well as visual; she heard Gwen's voice in her head, telling her not to be afraid.

PRACTICE 8: YOUR SOUND EXPERIENCES

If you've experienced spirit contact through a voice or some other type of sound, jot down what you remember about it. These questions might help:

- Were you frightened or energized?

- What were you thinking and feeling when it occurred?

- What age were you?

- How do you think the contact came about?

- After it occurred, did you tell anyone else about it? If not, why?

- Did you know the spirit?

- Have you had other contact with this same spirit?

- What message, if any, was imparted by the spirit?

It's beneficial to write down any spirit contact experience so you have a record of what happened. Over time, you may notice a pattern to these incidents. You might, for instance, discover that your contacts take place in a particular way or at a particular time of day or night. Perhaps sounds and scents are your clearest incidents of contact. If so, you'll be able to incubate an inner climate that's more receptive to this type of contact.

Keeping a record also deepens your intuition and heightens your awareness.

Scents

Contact through scents happens, but seems to be less common than contact through sounds. Perhaps this is because sounds come in many forms—booms, voices, knockings, music, crashes, thuds, clattering. Whatever it is, sounds in spirit contact usually aren't subtle. But scents are different and can be difficult to pigeonhole as a spirit contact unless the scent is one you associate with a loved one who has passed.

After Mike Perry's father died, he sometimes smelled tobacco smoke in the rooms of his home. No one in his household smoked, but his father used to smoke a pipe when he visited.

Trish's mother died not long after we moved in June 2000. We were cleaning out a storage unit where we'd stored some of our belongings and pieces of furniture and odds and ends that belonged to Trish's parents. As Trish was moving stuff to the front of the unit so we could load things on the dolly, she suddenly caught a whiff of her mother's perfume. It was a distinctive scent, something Rose Marie had worn on social occasions and holidays.

Her first thought was that the scent was embedded in her parents' belongings. But when the skin at the back of her neck prickled, she turned around, sensing her mother was with her. "Mom?"

The scent got a little stronger, as if in response, then began dissipating.

The challenge in researching this kind of contact is that it's easy for a skeptic—parent, partner, teacher, friend, sibling, stranger—to dismiss your experience as "your imagination," a remark that is often followed by laughter and derision. As a result, people who experience these encounters often don't want to talk about it for fear of being ridiculed. When you have been ridiculed frequently, it tends to erode your belief in your own experiences and you may close yourself off to further contact.

However, if your home environment is one that's open and receptive to these experiences, it makes all the difference. You can then be comforted by these experiences and talk about them without fear of being ridiculed.

In another example, Vicki's Italian in-laws made wine in the basement of the home they built. They used fruits from their garden, where they grew fig, apple, and pear trees. After they both passed, Vicki and her family started smelling freshly cut apples and pears when they were sitting in their living room.

"The smell moves. It will stay with one of us for a few moments, until we recognize it, then it will move to another person, then it will just be gone. The scent is so clearly that of freshly cut apples and pears!" Vicki's youngest daughter moved into the house while she was finishing college and whenever she caught the scent of apples and pears, she was comforted by it.

While recognizing a familiar scent related to a deceased loved one is the most obvious way spirit contact via scent manifests, sometimes location can come into play, especially if that location is a historical one. That's what we experienced during a visit to the Biltmore Estate in Asheville, North Carolina. The mansion is touted as the largest privately owned home in America. The mansion was built by George Washington Vanderbilt II between 1889 and 1895, has 250 rooms, and 178,926 square feet. The floor space covers four acres that include 33 bedrooms, 43 bathrooms, 65 fireplaces, and three kitchens. It isn't clear why anyone would need a home this large, but it certainly gives the resident ghosts plenty of space to roam.

The estate, owned today by Vanderbilt descendants, is actually a museum that showcases a way of life as lived by the Vanderbilt family near the turn of the twentieth century. The house is immaculate and furnished with priceless antiques. But it lacks all the modern conveniences we rely on today.

We took a trip to Asheville several years ago, and were astonished by the immensity of the estate. It's comparable to England's Highclere Castle, better known as Downton Abbey, thanks to the popular PBS drama. As you move through the rooms, you feel as if you're moving into the past. The aura is so strong that you expect to see a coterie of servants attending to the needs of wealthy heirs who dine every evening in formal attire. Apparently, some people have seen just that.

We didn't see any ghosts on our visit, but we did experience a contact through the scent of cigar smoke in the Biltmore library. Smoking isn't permitted in the house, but this odor was strong and so distinct that we almost expected to see gentlemen in top hats sitting around the coffee table puffing on stogies.

We moved on to another room where Trish asked a guard about the smoke. He sniffed at the air. "Yup, it's one of the ghosts. We smell cigar smoke from time to time."

Other employees at the Biltmore were dismissive about the idea of spirits inhabiting the place. But if you do an Internet search for *haunted Biltmore house,* former and present-day employees relate their experiences with encounters. They range from sounds and scents to deeply uncomfortable feelings and sensations in some of the rooms to actual sightings.

If the quantum physicists are correct and we're all interconnected, then this connection apparently includes spirits, whether we are aware of them or not.

PRACTICE 9: YOUR SCENT EXPERIENCES AND INTUITION CHECK

Once again, jot down any contact you've had through scents and smells. Be as detailed as possible. If you've had more than one experience, think about any patterns you may have noticed in terms of time of day, your moods, thoughts, feelings.

It's fascinating to read accounts of people's experiences in the Biltmore and in other haunted areas in the US. For the most part, these individuals aren't mediums or psychics trained to pick up energy from the deceased. They are ordinary people on vacation with family and friends. But put these people in a place that's reputedly haunted, and the wiring in their consciousness changes. It becomes intuitively primed to sense the unknown, the unusual, the mysterious.

Think about times when you have felt or sensed the possible presence of someone or something you can't see. How strong were the feelings?

Did goose bumps erupt on your arms? Did the back of your neck prickle? What physical sensations did you experience?

Intuition often registers first in the physical body or you experience it as an impulse to do or say something that seems out of character. Some people feel it as a burning sensation in the solar plexus, a tingling feeling in their fingers or teeth, or as a powerful hunch. How does it manifest for you?

Write in your journal about how your intuition comes into play when you suspect you are *about* to experience contact with the spirit world.

Sensations

Beyond subtle nudges from your intuition signaling contact with the other side is immanent, some people feel considerably more intense bodily sensations when contact is made. These feelings could range from disorientation and confusion to shock, depending on the circumstances.

Henry Flagler was a founding partner of Standard Oil and the earliest and undoubtedly the most important developer of Florida. He developed two million acres of land and his East Coast Railway connected the entire east coast of the state, from Jacksonville to Key West.

In 1902, when Flagler was sixty, he built Whitehall as a wedding gift for his third wife, twenty-four-year-old Mary Lily Kenan. The *New York Herald* declared that Henry Flagler's Gilded Age estate in Palm Beach was "more wonderful than any palace in Europe, grander and more magnificent than any other private dwelling in the world."[23] With seventy-five rooms, it isn't as large as the Biltmore and its grounds are considerably smaller. But its history is just as rich and mysterious, and much of it is preserved in the mansion, which today is called the Flagler Museum.

In the mid-1970s, our friends Bruce and Lynn Gernon were visiting the museum when she had an encounter with a man she believes was

---

23   Henry Morrison Flagler Museum, Palm Beach, FL, https://www.flaglermuseum .us/history/whitehall.

Flagler's ghost. She and Bruce were on the second floor and Lynn had gotten lost. She was looking for the restroom and ended up in one of the strange little hallways that lead to a room. And in this hallway, she encountered a man dressed in overalls. She asked him where the restroom was and he gestured off to his right. "Down there."

"I knew something strange was going on," Lynn said, describing the odd sensation that came over her. "I felt really disoriented, disconnected. I followed his directions toward the restroom and when I glanced back, he was gone." Bruce says that when he finally found Lynn, she was pale, scared, and it took a while for her to tell him what she'd experienced.

PRACTICE 10: YOUR SENSATION EXPERIENCES

Have you ever seen a spirit? If so, what were the conditions? Once again, jot down as many details as you can recall about the sighting, particularly how you felt at the time—your emotions, sensations, intuitive nudges, hunches. Was the sighting spontaneous? Or did you incubate an inner climate that made you more receptive to it? Did you request such a sighting?

Again, by recording such experiences, you're creating a record from which you can eventually discern patterns.

Empathic Encounters

This next example not only involved spirit contact through sensations, but involved several spirits and spanned a period of nearly twenty-five years.

Renie was a South Florida artist and psychic who often volunteered her services with the Cooper City Police. She was a tall, large-boned woman, a redhead with a kick-your-ass attitude who dominated any room she entered, any gathering she joined. She was opinionated, funny, stubborn, smart, and sassy. She was an ace astrologer who mentored

Trish, and a psychic with such raw talent that one Cooper City cop began to use her in his investigations.

In the summer of 1981, Renie and the cop were driving near a mall in Hollywood, Florida, where six-year-old Adam Walsh was last seen in Sears on July 27, 1981, shopping with his mother. The cop hoped Renie might be able to pick up something psychically about the missing boy—where he was, what had happened to him, if he'd been abducted.

At that point, the police believed he'd been abducted, but didn't have any leads. Renie didn't have an object that belonged to Adam, but heart-wrenching posters of the boy wearing his baseball uniform and cap were everywhere in South Florida. His huge, innocent eyes whispered, *I am your son, your brother, your cousin, your neighbor.* His face had been burned into the collective consciousness and that seemed to be all Renie needed.

When she and the cop were within a few miles of the mall, Renie's hands suddenly flew to her throat. She started choking, gasping for air. The cop had worked with her often enough to realize she was picking up something related to Adam and quickly sped away. Several miles later, he swerved to the side of the road.

"What is it, Renie?"

She sobbed. "Adam was decapitated."

It was as if Adam's spirit had reached out to Renie and her empathic ability enabled her to physically feel how he died.

Not long afterward, the head of the six-year-old boy was discovered in a canal in Vero Beach, Florida, more than a hundred miles north of the Hollywood mall. Ottis Toole, a serial killer, was serving five life sentences for murder when he confessed to killing Adam Walsh. He died of liver cancer in 1996 at the age of forty-nine. However, it wasn't until 2008 that police announced they had verified Toole's confession that he had killed John Walsh's son.

We observed Renie in action several years later, on a dismal, rainy night in late 1984. We drove with her to the police department in Greenacres, Florida, to see what she could pick up on regarding a missing girl. Eight-year-old Christie Luna had vanished near her home in Greenacres on May 24, 1984. Around three p.m., she had walked to a store to buy cat food and never returned. Police suspected foul play.

Renie had requested toys that Christie played with, her way of connecting with the girl's spirit. She sat on the floor of the police station clutching an old teddy bear, running her hands over it. Her eyes were shut as she rocked back and forth, humming softly. Everything about Renie at that moment suggested a small, childlike person. She started to whimper, then cry, then sob, her body hunched over the teddy bear.

"The mother's boyfriend used to beat her," Renie murmured. "She's deaf in one ear because of it." The deafness was later confirmed.

We left the station with the officer and drove around Greenacres, through the wet darkness. Christie's teddy bear was on Renie's lap as we passed the house where the girl had lived and the store where she was headed when she vanished. Renie directed us through streets until we came to a wooded area surrounded by a high wire-mesh fence. Renie disliked what she was feeling and turned to the officer. "You should search in there."

Renie felt the girl had been killed by the mother's boyfriend, but Christie Luna's body was never found and the case remained open.

Renie passed away in 2002. But in 2008, twenty-four years after she had clutched Christie Luna's teddy bear, both she and the case entered our lives again through a strange and startling synchronicity and spirit contact.

Dennie Gooding, a psychic in Los Angeles, called to say she was going to be in South Florida, and hoped we could get together. Nancy McMoneagle, director of the Monroe Institute in Virginia, where out-of-body experiences and the nature of consciousness are explored, also called and said she was going to be in South Florida the same weekend. As it turned out, they had both been invited by the wife of a detective who was investigating a cold case. They would be staying with her in Greenacres, which is less than ten miles from our home in Wellington. So we invited them both to come over one evening during their stay.

That morning we found an uncashed check for fifty dollars from Renie, dated 1987, with *loan repayment* printed at the bottom of it. We wondered where the check had been all these years. After all, we had moved twice since the check had been written and why had it suddenly turned up now? We didn't think about it until later that evening, when we were talking with Dennie.

"So what kind of case are you working on with this detective?" Trish asked.

She described the unsolved mystery of a girl from Greenacres who'd gone missing in 1984 and was presumed dead. "But her body has never been found."

Goose bumps crawled up Trish's arms. "You mean Christie Luna?"

Dennie looked shocked. "How'd you know that?"

Trish told her about Renie and that night twenty-four years earlier, then went over to a drawer and brought out the check from Renie.

"Synchronicity!" Dennie exclaimed.

Dennie wasn't able to locate Christie's body. But interestingly, when she and the cop in charge of the cold case were driving around, she pinpointed the same area that Renie had—several acres of yet-undeveloped, government-owned land, bordered by a metal fence. "I feel she's buried in there."

The synchronicities and instances of spirit contact in this confluence of events are startling. Something that began in 1984 came full circle on that night in 2008, twenty-four years later. Not only did Dennie pinpoint the same area that Renie had, but on the day we learned of Dennie's involvement in the case, we found the check Renie had written us decades ago. It was as if the spirits of both Renie and Christie Luna were urging us to pay attention, to acknowledge this contact between the living and the dead. *C'mon,* they seemed to be whispering. *You can solve this thing.*

Now and then, something appears in our local newspaper about the Christie Luna case. But as of May 2018, the case is still open.

PRACTICE 11: EMPATHIC SENSATIONS

Empaths pick up physical sensations and impressions that are sometimes quite literal, as Renie's were with both the Adam Walsh and Christy Luna cases. But an empath can also tune into moods, feelings, and emotional traumas of the living and of the dead. They can sense and feel the residue of intense emotions in places with a history—old hotels, museums, structures—where a violent event like a homicide has occurred.

When you enter old buildings, do you have distinct physical sensations about what has taken place there? If so, what kinds of sensations do you experience? Do you feel the presence of spirits?

Can you easily tune in on other people's moods and emotions? Some empaths are like psychic sponges who absorb the energy of the people around them. If you fit that ticket, then you already know why it's so important to associate with positive, upbeat people.

Renie Wiley's ability had been part of her life since a near-death experience during childbirth. But the talents of some empaths develop over time. If you work in a profession, for instance, where you counsel people or work in some facet of the health or medical field, then empathic ability grows out of your continued interaction with clients and patients.

Once you're aware of this ability within yourself, you can learn to direct and mold it to include tuning in to spirits, particularly your ancestors.

Practice 12: Tuning In to Ancestors

Think back over your family history. Do you know any dramatic stories from generations ago that have been passed down? Ask older family members and relatives. Select someone who suffered some sort of family tragedy. How do you feel about it? Know that you have the ability to send healing energy to the spirit.

Begin by surrounding yourself in a protective white or gold light, or any other method to shield you from any invasive contact. Relax and meditate on the person in question, and attempt to tune into his or her life.

Use your empathy to get a sense of how the person might've felt about a particular matter. Perhaps it involved the loss of a child, or a setback of some sort. By sending love and positive energy, you can help heal old wounds. Also, express your gratitude for any reciprocating energy that is sent your way from this spirit and other ancestors. Focus on balancing the energy so both sides will benefit.

You might encounter resistance and an unwillingness to participate in the exchange of energy. In that case, thank the spirit for the encounter, however brief, and release the contact. Know that you have made a positive impact, even though it might not feel that way.

5

❋

Animal Signs
& Symbols

ANIMALS APPEAR FREQUENTLY as messengers in synchronicities that alert us about a life occurrence, people, or an event that are about to enter our experience. Not surprisingly, animals also act as messengers from Spirit and while the details may vary, the larger picture is remarkably consistent. A loved one passes away and the family and friends left behind begin to see a particular animal for whom the deceased felt a special affinity.

In 2010, when Darren of Australia was married and had two young sons, he experienced a remarkable animal spirit contact. His father-in-law, John, had died of a sudden heart attack several days earlier, and he and his wife were spending a lot of time with her mother.

"He loved to feed the wild parrots, magpies, kookaburras, and other birds that would drop by his house every day," Darren says. "They actually sat near his veranda railing, waiting to be fed. Shortly after John's death, my mother-in-law was telling us all how he loved it when the parrots would do their mating dance. He would imitate the male, who would wobble up behind the female and then flap its wings up and down (a bit like a dirty old man flapping his raincoat). This would send him into hysterics."

Darren considered telling his mother-in-law that they should be alert for a sign from John that involved a parrot because he often joked about coming back as one, even though he believed when you were dead, that was it. But his mother-in-law, like Darren's wife, was skeptical about life after death, so Darren didn't say anything.

"My mother-in-law had the TV on, a distraction from the sadness and raw emotion she was feeling. It was tuned to *Australia's Funniest Home Videos* and what should come on but two parrots trying their mating dance on an artificial parrot! What are the *odds?*"

Darren's wife and mother-in-law found great comfort in the synchronicity. Darren felt John was communicating with them that he was alive and well on the other side.

Any animal can act as a spirit messenger when we, the living, are aware and open to the possibility. Otherwise, the potential messenger may be dismissed as an oddity or overlooked altogether. Sometimes, though, the messenger is so up close and personal it can't be ignored.

The Bat

In late 2015, Jane Clifford, a healer and psychic in Wales, lost her closest friend of forty years. Three days after her friend died, Jane was on the phone with a clairvoyant who told her she would have a meaningful encounter with an animal that would be her friend's spirit communicating with her.

As they talked, a bat flew through an open window and into Jane's living room. It circled gracefully through the room for half an hour and didn't seem distressed or anxious. For Jane, the appearance of that bat, at that exact moment, was an absolute confirmation her friend was alive and well on the other side.

For many of us, a bat flying into our home might prompt us to run after it with a broom and try to shoo it back outside. But Jane understood the synchronicity of the event, and was struck by how the bat appeared just as the clairvoyant was predicting an encounter with an animal.

The esoteric meaning of bats varies. Among Native Americans, they're regarded as guides through darkness, death, and re-birth. The Mayans had a bat god called Camazote, who was believed to test human souls with a sword. Its connotation was negative because of the implied violence. They are blind, but because of their ability to echo-locate, are expert navigators. In some esoteric traditions, they are associated with understanding grief, camouflage, invisibility, clairaudience—the ability to hear sounds from other dimensions—and the ability to sense what others can't. The Chinese regard them as a symbol of happiness.

In his classic book, *Animal Speak*, Ted Andrews wrote: "The bat is one of the most misunderstood mammals. Modern depictions in movies and television have given it a sinister reputation, but it plays an important role in Nature and as a symbol in totem traditions—Native American tribes that prized sacred objects that symbolized a family, lineage, or clan. Although more modern lore places the bat in cohorts with the devil, with its dragon-like wings, in more ancient times it was a powerful symbol." [24]

Birds

Hummingbirds

The number of bird species on the planet varies according to different sources. According to the International Ornithologists' Union, there are 10,500 known species and 21,000 subspecies. In a 2011 issue of *Mother Jones* magazine [25], the actual number of birds was cited as between two hundred and four hundred billion worldwide, with ten to twenty

---

24   Ted Andrews. *Animal Speak: The Spiritual & Magical Powers of Creatures Great & Small* (S. Paul, MN: Llewellyn, 2002), 248.

25   Kevin Drum. "How Many Birds?" Mother Jones, http://www.motherjones.com /kevin-drum/2011/03/how-many-birds, May 23, 2011.

billion just in the US. Regardless of the exact number, birds exist on every continent and perhaps because they are so numerous, they figure prominently in many spirit contact stories. Quite often, these experiences happen spontaneously. In some way, they reflect the situation or personality of the spirit—as with John's enjoyment of wild parrots—or trigger a memory in the experiencer that's connected to the deceased.

Recently, for instance, Trish was texting her sister, Mary, about some old family photos she had found of their parents. These pictures dated back to their childhood in Venezuela, when their parents were in their late forties and Trish and Mary were youngsters. While Trish waited for Mary to respond, she glanced out her office window into the lush tropical yard just as a pair of gorgeous hummingbirds flitted past and hovered over a large, flowering bush.

We rarely see hummingbirds in South Florida and in the eighteen years we have lived in this house, have never seen one—much less two—in our yard. The sight of them reminded Trish that about the time the photos were taken, her dad had won a weeklong trip to Barbados for the entire family. One of the highlights of that trip was a hummingbird that stopped by every afternoon at precisely 4 p.m. to hover above a tea-time sugar bowl on the porch table. They were all fascinated by its lack of fear, its beauty, and its punctuality. With that memory, Trish felt certain the hummingbirds embodied the spirits of her parents, who were dropping in to say hi.

Sandy, a retired veterinarian, experienced a cluster of hummingbird synchronicities that seemed to be telling her that her beloved dog, Nellie, might be ailing.

In August 2013, Nellie was thirteen and not eating well, and just wasn't herself. One night, Sandy had a magnificent dream about two hummingbirds hovering around her mailbox, facing each other. They were larger than normal hummingbirds and she sensed they were mates. In the dream, their wings came together to form a heart shape.

A couple of days after the dream, she and her husband were sitting in their yard and a hummingbird appeared, larger than most hummingbirds, just as in her dream. She noted that hummingbirds are winter residents in Florida and it was mid-August. She had no idea what a hummingbird was doing there at that time of year. To Sandy, hummingbirds represented angelic energy, and joy.

A few days later, she was downloading songs her friend had sent her years ago. She figured she should get them into the music file on her computer. While the songs downloaded, she noticed a hummingbird out in the garden and went over to the window to get a closer look. But it had flown away. She turned back to her computer and saw that the download had stalled. The song that refused to download? Seals & Crofts's "Hummingbird."

The next day, Sandy passed a road she'd never seen before and glanced at the sign: Hummingbird Lane. It was now abundantly clear to her that she was in the grips of synchronicity and she felt it related to Nellie's deterioration. Sandy checked her over and found a large mass in her abdomen. She took the dog to her vet, and sure enough, he identified it as well. He didn't think Nellie was a candidate for surgery and not long afterward, Sandy and George had to put her down.

Sandy understood the cluster of hummingbird synchros had been alerting her to Nellie's condition. Hummingbirds not only symbolize joy, but in some indigenous traditions are considered messengers from the spirit world. The synchros softened the blow of her dog's passing, and helped to heal their broken hearts.

This story begs the question: Did Nellie's soul summon these hummingbirds so Sandy would realize Nellie wasn't just ailing, but was dying? Can a pet's soul call on other creatures—even those of a different species—and enlist their help in the process of dying?

Perhaps. As author Dean Koontz writes in *A Big Little Life: A Memoir of a Joyful Dog Named Trixie,* "Living with a recognition of the spiritual dimension of the world not only ensures a happier life but also a more honest intellectual life than if we allow no room for wonder and refuse to acknowledge the mystery of existence." [26]

In our exploration of spirit contact, we've heard some truly bizarre and wondrous stories. But one, which also involves a hummingbird, is one of the strangest. It suggests communication from ancient spirits, specifically the spirit of the artist who created the hummingbird figure on the Nazca Lines in Peru.

Years ago, William was living in a mother-in-law-style apartment attached to a house outside Scottsdale, Arizona. The place had a lot of windows that looked out onto a grove of lovely oak trees.

It was a gorgeous, sunny afternoon and William was lying on a couch downstairs in a room with big windows. He was near the open door that led out to the patio. He was reading one of Paul Devereux's books, *Shamanism and the Mystery Lines,* in which the author discussed the Nazca Lines in Peru. He wondered to himself about the humming- bird figure that someone had created on the Nazca plain. The graphic, he thought, was strikingly visual, but he'd never seen a hummingbird in anything like that particular position.

The Nazca image, which you can find online, shows a hummingbird positioned with its beak stretched to the front and its wings extended to the side, an unusual position for a hummingbird. When most of us see one of these birds, it's in perpetual motion, wings humming, fluttering almost too quickly for the eye to see.

The Nazca image, William said, was beautiful, "But it struck me that the position of the bird is so unnatural and I remember feeling stumped at how the artist came up with that curious interpretation. I've taken a num- ber of college-level art classes, including life drawing and art history, so I'm familiar with the process. Wondering got me nowhere fast. As I stood

---

26   Dean Koontz. *A Big Little Life: a memoir of a joyful dog named Trixie.* (New York: Hyperion, 2009), 263.

up to go to the fridge for some cheese, I heard a buzzing sound. Looking toward the sound, I saw that a little male Anna's Hummer had gotten into the house and was trying to leave by flying through the window."

The hummingbird was engaged in the same actions as a bug struggling to escape a window, staying close to the glass at the edge of the window and slowly moving up and down, wings a blur. "The angle formed by the edge of the window made it easy for me to slowly approach the little hummingbird and close my hands around his body, all the while saying: *'Let me love you, let me love you.'* I wanted to convey my intent, though I'm sure my heart was beating as fast as his!

"I walked outside a few steps and opened my hands to let the hummingbird fly off. I looked down as I lifted my right hand to see the hummingbird lying prone in the palm of my left hand. It was positioned with beak stretched out to the front and wings extended to each side." Exactly like the hummingbird image on the Nazca plain.

Within a second or two, the hummingbird realized he could fly away and did. William was left with a burning question: Under what circumstance did the ancient artist hold a live hummingbird in his or her hands? But even more to the point, did the hummingbird that entered William's home embody the ancient spirit of the artist who had created that image? Had William's state of mind as he read *Shamanism and the Mystery Lines* created an inner climate that was conducive to this kind of contact?

This inner climate, whether it's created consciously or unconsciously, is vital in spirit contact. Sometimes we have the luxury of inviting this climate into our lives. But other times, we're caught or trapped in situations where we're desperate for answers, signs, something that can guide, enlighten, confirm, or warn us about decisions we should make, directions we should move toward. These situations frequently involve pivotal events in our lives. Whether to move or not. Marriage or divorce. Life or death. And when the choices are either/or, black or white, this is when the owl may make an appearance.

Owls

In the Harry Potter movies, owls fly through the cafeteria at Hogwarts, delivering mail, dropping letters in front of the characters who define these novels. The owls are creatures that traverse the boundary between the ordinary world and the world of magic. It's the perfect visual for the archetypal energy of owls as messengers. Regardless of culture or belief, owls are often seen as messengers of some sort—between man and the spirit world, as in shamanic traditions; between humans and aliens, as in encounter experiences; and between the living and the dead.

In the lives of ordinary people, they can be any or all of the above.

For a decade or so, we lived on a lake that was frequented by all kinds of birds. A family of burrowing owls had been attracted to the lake and nested in our backyard. They are small, sandy-colored owls with bright yellow eyes that live in underground burrows they've dug or have taken from other creatures. The species is endangered and in South Florida, where the owls often make ground nests near schools or other public places, the areas are protected to prevent people from disturbing their nests.

We had several experiences with these owls, the first occurring shortly after we'd returned from a trip to New York. We had met with our agent and had dinner with Richard "Fids" Demian, a talented psychic we'd known for years. We were in the kitchen, talking about Fids, when we suddenly heard the high-pitched screech of some burrowing owls. We hurried outside, puzzled by why they were flying around in the afternoon. Dusk was usually their time of day. One of the owls touched down on an eave just above our front door and stayed there awhile, hooting softly.

We knew about owl symbolism and were concerned about what the owl above the door might mean. That evening, we received a call telling us Fids had been found in his apartment that afternoon, dead of a heart attack.

As nearly as we can figure, our sighting of the owl and our talk about Fids occurred at about the time his body was found. It's one of the clearest spirit messenger experiences we've ever had with any bird or animal.

Belief in the idea that birds—or other animals—can act as spirit messengers isn't necessarily a prerequisite for experiencing such an encounter. Sometimes, these things happen in such bizarre and unusual ways you can't dismiss them as meaningless. During the time Barbara interned in New York City in 2000, working for the Al Gore campaign, a friend she interned with told her an owl story that always stuck with her.

Her friend's grandfather had died during the semesters she interned and shortly afterward, the young man got married to his college sweetheart. "At their outdoor reception, a baby screech owl watched from a tree branch and didn't move one bit, even with the loud live band playing! My friend saw it as a good omen that his grandfather's spirit was watching over the festivities. And he didn't believe in such things."

These kinds of experiences are especially comforting to people in the hours, days, or weeks after the death of a loved one, when emotions are so raw. In fact, this emotional state may create the inner climate that's necessary for the experience to occur. We want so badly to believe that our loved one is still with us and can hear us, see us, sense us, that we're more open and receptive when it actually happens.

When Leah lost her grandfather, an event we discussed in chapter 3, she was devastated. She'd been particularly close to him. A few weeks after he died, Leah was sitting in the kitchen with her grandmother and her friend, Linda, when an owl chime suddenly started chiming like crazy. "Owls were gram's favorite animal, which is why I think my grandfather chose that one. It rang like mad for a few minutes, until

Linda said, 'Hi Mr. Mitchell.' And that was it. I was blown away and so grateful he stopped by."

Over a period of four years, Leah lost three grandparents and her dad. "The loss has been overwhelming for us. But these occurrences help that feeling of emptiness and the synchronicities assure me they are still around me."

There are times when experiences with animals seem to be pre-cognitive, almost as if the spirit of the individual knows of the body's impending demise and reaches out to loved ones to prepare them. This may happen when a disease like Alzheimer's or dementia is involved, or when brain function is impaired in some way. The person's soul or spirit may already have moved on, but the body is still alive.

During the last several years of Trish's mother's life, Rose Marie was in an Alzheimer's unit and her dad, Tony, lived with us. Rose Marie had occasional periods of lucidity, but for the most part, she lived in a kind of netherworld, a place of make believe. She claimed that her brothers and sisters (all dead) visited her, and that her own mother—who had died in 1969, the day Armstrong walked on the moon—had brought her dinner or stopped by to play bridge.

One Sunday afternoon, our daughter, Megan, came racing into the kitchen, shouting about a burrowing owl perched on the atrium fence outside Tony's bedroom. We immediately thought the owl's appearance might be a portent of some sort. The fact that the owl was perched on the fence in broad daylight—odd behavior for an owl—puzzled us.

We stood at the sliding glass door, gawking at the owl. Then we noticed the bird was perched on just one leg. We thought the left leg might just be pulled up, so we hurried outside for a closer look. It wasn't the least bit startled as we approached. We realized its left leg wasn't just pulled up; part of its leg was missing.

At nine the next morning, the phone rang. It was the Alzheimer's facility, alerting us that Rose Marie was on the way to the ER, presumably for a broken hip. We rushed over to the hospital and found her in excruciating pain. X-rays were taken, doctors arrived and left. By the end of the day, the prognosis was worse than a broken hip. Rose Marie's left hip bone—the same leg that was missing on the owl—had disintegrated completely. She wasn't a candidate for a hip replacement because she didn't have the presence of mind necessary for the rehab.

Rose Marie was transferred to a nursing home, where pain management consisted of regular doses of morphine. She died three weeks later of pneumonia. It seemed the owl had served as a messenger of what was soon to come.

Geese

Canada geese are large waterfowl with black heads and necks, white patches on their faces, and bodies that are usually tan or brown. They adapt well in urban areas, especially in habitats close to water and in grassy fields. They may also be found on your front lawn, since grass is easy for them to digest, and wide expanses of lawn give them an unobstructed view of approaching predators. Like 90 percent of bird species, they mate for life.

A few years ago, a man wrote us about a spirit contact he experienced with Canada geese he found uplifting and odd. The day before Easter, Robin and his wife went by the cemetery to place flowers on his parents' graves. The cemetery is located along a busy highway outside Chicago. The area is urban, lacking ponds, lakes, or any other body of water, and there aren't any grain fields or lawns that might attract waterfowl or other wildlife. "But there at my family's grave sites were two Canada geese waddling around very regally and purposefully. With no water, food, or other attractant in the vicinity, this was strangely comical—sort of like finding a buffalo or aardvark or something wandering around a mausoleum—it struck me as that incongruous. They stayed nearby, practically underfoot, while we visited and arranged the flowers on the headstone."

When they later drove away, Robin remembered Canada geese mate for life and the symbolism struck him. "My mother and father spent their lives together and my grieving mother died within six months of my father's passing. This pair of geese: were they there that day to highlight their memory?" Or were they there as spirit messengers, letting Robin know his parents were still together and doing well in the afterlife?

PRACTICE 13: YOUR ANIMAL INVENTORY

Before we move on to other critters, let's take an inventory of your awareness of animals as messengers. Take note of which statements apply to you.

1. I frequently have experiences with animal messengers.

2. I rarely have experiences with animal messengers.

3. I don't believe animals can be messengers from the spirit world.

4. I believe that spirit contact is possible through animal messengers.

5. My spirit contact happens primarily in dreams where an animal figures prominently, or in a combination of dreams and actual encounters with animals.

6. My pets often act as spirit messengers.

7. I meditate and during my meditations, animals come to me with messages.

8. I have an animal totem.

9. I enjoy being in nature and some of my best animal encounters happen there.

10. I cultivate an inner climate for spirit contact through animals, through meditation, receptivity, and awareness of my environment.

11. I keep a journal about spirit contact.

Keeping a journal of such experiences is a great way to build a kind of database about what particular animals symbolize for you. It's wise to date each experience, so you have a frame of reference, and to briefly describe where the experience happened and your state of mind at the time. Were you more open and receptive than usual? Were you thinking about a deceased loved one when the experience occurred? How did you feel as it was happening? The more detail you include, the more valuable your database becomes.

Dogs & Cats

According to the ASPCA, dog and cat ownership in the US is estimated at 78 million dogs and 85.8 million cats.[27] Many of them aren't just pets, but are members of the family. And when we lose our animal buddies, they often hang around in spirit and communicate in some way that they are still with us.

When Trish's mother was near the end of her life, we were asked if we would adopt a golden retriever. We had two cats at the time and no intention of getting a dog, but decided to try Jessie out for a couple of days and see how she got along with our cats.

Jessie walked into the house, greeted the cats with her tail wagging, and found a spot in Megan's bedroom and, later, in front of Rob's desk. She was with us for nearly twelve wonderful years. Our cats loved her; our parrot, a dusky conure, often rode around on her back; and like many retrievers, she was a people dog. People adored her.

After Trish's mother moved into an Alzheimer's unit, we took Jessie with us for visits. None of the residents ever remembered our names, but they always remembered Jessie's. The day before Trish's mother died in a nursing home, Jessie went with us for what turned out to be our last visit. Even though Rose Marie was unconscious, we felt that she sensed

---

27   "Shelter Intake and Surrender: Pet Statistics, ASPCA. https://www.aspca.org /animal-homelessness/shelter-intake-and-surrender/pet-statistics, 2017.

Jessie's presence. At one point, her hand dropped onto Jessie's head and Jessie licked it and Rose Marie sighed as if to thank us for bringing Jessie to see her.

Around 2005, Jessie developed problems swallowing and our vet discovered a tumor in her throat. She had surgery and the tumor was removed. Although the vet said he'd gotten all of it, the tumor was malignant and he warned us it might grow back. In the spring of 2007, we noticed she occasionally had trouble walking. But the vet couldn't find anything wrong with her.

In June of that year, we took her with us to move Megan out of her college dorm and back home for the summer. During the ride, Jessie seemed lethargic, worn out, and by the time we got to Sarasota, couldn't even get out of the car on her own. Alarmed, we took her to the vet the next day and were told the tumor had grown back and the cancer had spread. We had to have her put down, one of the saddest days of our lives.

For months afterward, we heard the tap of her claws against the wooden floors as her spirit followed us around the house. Several times, when we were sitting on the couch watching TV or lying in bed, the cushions or the mattress would suddenly move and a depression would form. We knew she was with us and suspected the cats could see her. Several times, our white cat, Powder, would rub her head up against the air, just as she used to rub her head against Jessie's snout or body, and would purr with contentment.

People who have lost dogs report a variety of signs that the dog's spirit is still with them—noises, scents, a toy the dog once played with falls out of a cabinet or off of a shelf. Spirit contact through or from animals takes many different forms. But with pet dogs and cats, animals who have shared our lives, the contact is often layered and unfolds over days or weeks.

Natalie Thomas, a medium in Australia, says when she's doing readings for clients, she sometimes picks up on their deceased animal companions and this serves as confirmation for the client that she is actually tuning in to the afterlife. Several years ago, Natalie was working at a fundraiser and a lady sat down for a reading. "I told her that a powerful energy was coming through who was saying he loved her and thanking her for loving him. She asked the person's name, and all I got was the word 'Frog'. I asked her if it was someone's nickname and she burst into tears."

It turned out that Frog was a Staffordshire terrier who had belonged to one of the woman's friends. He was quite wild, so the friend had given him away because she couldn't care for him. "He kept jumping my client's fence, hence the name 'Frog'. The trouble was because he was a Staffy, he kept hurting himself trying to get over the top of the fence as it was really too high for him. My client had cared for him and loved him as much as any human could and in return he was watching over her from the other side and sent his love through me." It was a powerful experience for both the client and for Natalie and a confirmation that our animal companions, just like our human loved ones, live on after death.

W. Bruce Cameron's wonderful book, *A Dog's Purpose: A Novel for Humans,* is told from the point of view of a dog, Bailey, who begins life as a golden retriever with a boy, Ethan, and his family. Bailey was with this family until Ethan was a young man and when he passed away, Ethan was with him, whispering that he would be missed, that he was loved. Then, suddenly, Bailey was back as a female German shepherd and worked with police, tracking down bad guys.

The book follows Bailey through several more lives until, in his final life, he's reunited with Ethan, now in his forties. Even though Bailey has a different dog body, Ethan recognizes him when he tosses a Frisbee and leans forward and the dog leaps onto his back and grabs the Frisbee from midair, a trick Bailey used to do when Ethan was a kid.

A Dog's Purpose is fiction, but … is it possible that our animal companions return to us?

Research on human reincarnation abounds. But for reincarnation in animals, there's only anecdotal evidence—the intuitive certainty we feel when confronted with an animal that may be the reincarnation of a beloved pet.

When Trish was in graduate school, she adopted a Himalayan cat from an animal shelter in Florida. His left eye was a milky color, scar tissue from an old injury where a claw had penetrated it, rendering him blind in that eye.

Trish named him Demian, after a character in a Hermann Hesse novel by the same name. He moved all over Florida with her, endured her prepublication rants, and rejoiced with her the day she sold her first novel in 1984. He was her feline buddy. Even on road trips, he perched on the top of the driver's seat, his body spread out so that at least one of his paws rested against her shoulder.

When we got married, Demian was delighted to have another man in the house. He sat in Rob's lap when he wrote, slept on Rob's side of the bed at night, and followed him around. Rob nicknamed him Doolittle, and the name stuck.

Around the time Demian Doolittle hit fourteen, he developed kidney problems. The vet said we could opt for dialysis until a kidney became available, and the transplant would have to take place in Atlanta, at a facility that performed them. We brought Doolittle home, babied him for a few days, discussing our options. In the end, we didn't want to subject him to all these medical procedures and returned to the vet's for euthanasia.

Anyone who has owned a pet they have to put down knows what this is like. There's a moment when your beloved pet looks at you, stretches a paw to touch your arm, licks the back of your hand, locks eyes with you, and you know that he knows. You feel his consciousness touching yours and you're choked up and want to scream, *Stop the IV, stop this, stop, we've changed our minds.* But you don't say a word. The animal makes some small, final sound.

Some people say they've seen the soul of their pet as it leaves the body, a pale wisp like smoke. Others just feel the soul's departure. That's how it was with Doolittle.

We buried him on the property of the condo where we lived at the time. About four months after his death, Trish dreamed she went into the kitchen to find something to eat, and Doolittle was at his bowl, chowing down. "Doolittle," she exclaimed in the dream. "What're you doing here? You're dead."

He raised his head and regarded her with that single clear blue eye. "Not really. And I'm coming back. You'll know me."

She felt the dream was Demian Doolittle's way of telling her that he was moving on, returning, preparing himself for whatever would come next in his scheme of things.

The next day, Trish scoured the newspaper for a kitten for sale. She took the dream Demian Doolittle at his word, figured the rebirth had happened already, and came home with a beautiful female tabby kitten, Fox, who was with us for a decade. But that cat wasn't Demian Doolittle.

Skip ahead several years to when we adopted Jessie, the golden retriever. We took her to the vet for her shots and during the exam, the vet said she had scar tissue of some sort in her left eye. It didn't affect her vision, but it was there and we should be aware of it.

Physical evidence that goes from life to life is well documented in humans. Dr. Ian Stevenson, a psychiatrist who taught for years at the University of Virginia, collected more than 2,500 cases. Author and past-life researcher Carol Bowman wrote about this in her book, *Return from Heaven.*[28] There's nothing documented about it among animals, but Trish felt certain that Jessie was Demian Doolittle, reincarnated. In

---

28   Carol Bowman. *Return from Heaven: Beloved Relatives Reincarnated Within Your Family.* New York: Bantam, 2003.

all, this animal soul was with us for twenty-five years. Now, every time Trish feeds a stray cat or dog or bird, she asks, *Hey, Doo, is it you?* She's still waiting for a definitive answer. A bark, a meow, a tweet, a voice.

Insects

Fireflies

Fireflies or lightning bugs are among the most magical insects. On warm summer nights, they flit around in the dark, their little bodies lit up with what scientists call "cold" light because the incandescence doesn't emit any heat. They thrive in tropical regions, but during the summer can be found on every continent except Antarctica.

Esoterically, when they are regarded as animal totems, they are symbolic of inspiration and hope. This is certainly what author David Morrell discovered when his fifteen-year-old son, Matthew, died of a rare form of cancer, Ewing's sarcoma. Nothing is more devastating for a parent than to lose a child. Our children, after all, are supposed to outlive us.

In *Fireflies,* his semifictionalized account of his son's illness, death, and the aftermath, he writes movingly of his son's terrible, agonizing journey and his own desperate attempts to save him. The night after the funeral, David went into his son's room and sank down on the bed. Suddenly the room was filled with fireflies and he heard his son say, "Don't be sad, Dad. I'm well now, and I can play!" [29]

Fireflies as spirit messengers may be more common than we think. A writer friend, Carol Gorman, shared her own beliefs concerning spirit contact came about as an experience she had in 1981. "My son George was six. I had recently been divorced from George's dad. My ex's father had died, and it was the night after his funeral. Anyway, he and I had never had any closure because my ex and I had split up, and I'd never seen him again.

29　David Morrell. *Fireflies.* (New York: Dutton, 1988), 178.

"I used to lie down on the bed with George at night as he was falling asleep. We'd lie in the dark and talk about his day. So that night, I said, 'Let's say a prayer, and I think Grandpa will hear us and know that we miss him.' So I said the prayer, and immediately after the prayer was over, I saw sparkles of what looked like static electricity in the air. I even heard the pops and crackles. It only lasted a few seconds and stopped. I wondered if I had imagined it. 'George, did you see the lights in here just now?' I asked. George replied, 'What lights?' So I assumed I'd imagined it. I'd never heard of this before."

Ten years later, Carol read David Morrell's book, *Fireflies*. Even though she hadn't heard a voice that night in George's room, she was struck by Morrell's description and how similar it was to what she'd experienced. "So I tucked it away in my mind, thinking maybe the static electricity was like David Morrell's fireflies."

Six or eight years later, Carol was writing novels for young readers and was invited to a book signing in a small-town library with David Morrell. "Nobody came, so I had the pleasure of sitting with David for a couple of hours. I told him I'd read his book *Fireflies* and described my experience with the lights in the room after the prayer.

"He nodded and said, 'That's exactly what I saw.' And he told me that everywhere he went to lecture after the publication of his book, someone in the room would raise a hand and say that something similar had happened to him/her. He said that a Catholic priest who counsels grieving people wrote him after reading *Fireflies* and told him that about 85% of the people he counsels report contact with the person who had died."

This experience introduced Carol to a new kind of spirituality, different from the Presbyterian religion she'd grown up with. "I wish everyone could have these experiences, so they know that life goes on and they don't have to be afraid of death."

Butterflies

Butterflies have long been symbols of transformation, metamorphosis, renewal, and rebirth. After all, they begin their lives as caterpillars, the homeliest of creatures, and after days or weeks in a cocoon, emerge as the loveliest of creatures. When they act as spirit messengers, they often reflect whatever is going on in a person's life at the moment of the encounter, as in Mike Perry's experience.

At the funeral of his closest friend, Mike was surprised to see a butterfly touch down on the coffin as it was carried into the church. The butterfly remained on top of the coffin throughout the service and Mike felt certain that the beautiful creature was his friend, checking in on his own funeral.

When we think about animals as spirit messengers, we probably assume the animals are large or they can fly or they have some overwhelming physical presence as predators. But insects can also be spirit messengers and sometimes in direct, startling ways.

Beetles and Ladybugs

In terms of size, the ladybug isn't much larger than an ant. But such an abundance of folklore exists about this creature that it must be because she's so much cuter than other bugs.

Back in the Middle Ages, for instance, farmers considered the ladybug to be a harbinger of good luck for the harvest because she consumed many of the insects that infested their crops. One popular legend about ladybugs concerns a village in centuries past whose fields were being threatened by hordes of insects. The villagers prayed for help and, in the eleventh hour, swarms of ladybugs arrived and saved their fields from destruction.

It's said that finding a ladybug is good luck and that it's *really* good luck if the ladybug lands on you. Killing a ladybug, of course, brings bad luck and sickness. In terms of spirit communication, the ladybug generally points to good fortune, harvest, and positive transformation.

Ladybugs love South Florida. They particularly like our local dog park. It consists of about five acres divided up for dogs of various sizes. Since our golden retriever Noah weighs more than one hundred pounds, we take him to the large dog park and usually end up sitting at a picnic table beneath a sprawling umbrella of trees. Noah prowls around, sniffing for squirrels, while all sorts of wildlife drop in for a visit. Squirrels, of course, but also wild parrots and a lot of bugs.

Usually, ladybugs are drawn to this picnic table and to whoever is sitting there. One afternoon, shortly after we heard that our friend Ed Gorman was in hospice, Trish was reading an e-mail from Carol, Ed's wife, about his deteriorating condition. She suddenly felt something crawling up her leg.

It was a ladybug. Trish reached down with her finger extended and the ladybug crawled onto it. Trish brought her hand up and rested it against the table. The ladybug stayed on her finger while she finished reading Carol's e-mail about Ed. Then the ladybug crawled off her finger onto the table and flew off. Trish felt it was Ed's spirit letting her know that his death would be peaceful.

If you talk about this kind of experience in the company of people whose beliefs differ from yours, you'll get weird looks. Or laughter. Or derision. Or all of the above. But none of that should ever prevent you from honoring your own experiences as valid and true. And it was fitting that Ed would choose the ladybug for this contact, a symbol of good fortune. He was always so generous with other writers, commissioning them to write pieces for *Mystery Scene,* the magazine he edited, offering advice about agents and editors, and putting them in touch with book packagers searching for ghostwriters. It fit.

PRACTICE 14: EXPLORING THE ANIMAL CONNECTION

Think about encounters you've had with animals. Did any of them occur when a loved one was dying or shortly after someone died? How did you feel at the time? Did you recognize the encounter as a spirit contact? Jot down in your journal any encounters you remember and what you learned from them. Be as specific as possible about time, location, your emotions, and the circumstances under which the encounter occurred.

6

✷

Cluster
Communication

THE DICTIONARY DEFINITION of cluster is straightforward: *a number of things of the same kind, growing or held together; a bunch.* When we talk about synchronicity clusters that don't involve spirit contact, we're referring to groups of numbers, objects, names, words, songs, objects, and events that are repeated over and over again. Usually, the repetition stops when we get whatever the message is.

During a flight to California some years ago, we noticed the number thirty-three kept popping up. Aisle 33, seat 33, flight 233. In a period of seven hours, we noted half a dozen recurrences of the number. We didn't have any idea what it meant. Trish finally turned to the *I Ching,* an ancient Chinese oracle that consists of sixty-four hexagrams, and looked up hexagram thirty-three. As soon as she saw the title— Retreat—she understood the message.

At the time, Trish's mother, Rose Marie, was in an Alzheimer's unit, in room 33. We were "in retreat" from that situation. We interpreted this cluster of synchronicities as confirmation that we had made the right choice in taking a break. Once we got the message, we no longer saw the number.

When spirit contact comes through clusters, it often involves the same numbers, objects, music, or whatever, but not always. Sometimes, the contact itself is the cluster, repeated contact over a period of days or weeks.

Angel in My Pocket

For thirty-five years, Russell, a cinematographer in Los Angeles, was involved with Trudy, a lawyer. Their relationship had gone through many permutations over the years, but they always remained close. When he died unexpectedly in 2009, Trudy felt lost without him. She didn't know how to fill the void his death left in her life.

Then, days after he died, she started noticing signs she felt indicated Russell was initiating contact with her. The first incident involved a lamp Trudy's sister had given her. It was filled with seashells and reminded her of the summers she and Russell had spent on Martha's Vineyard. Around midnight one night, the lamp turned on and the light awakened her. Yet she was certain she'd turned the lamp off before going to bed. It had never happened before.

"I was suddenly sure it was Russell."

When Trudy was cleaning out Russell's apartment, she decided to make a time capsule from letters and old photos, both professional and personal, that she found in his belongings. Another photographer was also there helping. One of the items she selected for the time capsule was an ID tag from a movie he had worked on. It was a favorite movie of his and the ID tag had been pinned to a bulletin board for the last seven years. When Trudy plucked it off the board to include it in the time capsule, she discovered the tag had a tiny LED light on it and the light was turned on.

She called the photographer over to take a look and he insisted it had come on because she'd touched it. But it remained on for two days until she sent the time capsule to the place where Russell's ashes were going to be buried. The day before the memorial service, they opened the time capsule again. The light was off. "You actually had to latch the little pin on the back to make it blink. It still gives me chills to think of that day. I'm *sure* Russell turned it on."

The two incidents with lights convinced Trudy that Russell was around. Then a third event occurred. Russell's upstairs neighbor had made a clock for him out of copper. It had tiny lights on it that blinked at 12, 3, 6, and 9 o'clock. It wasn't blinking when she cleaned out his studio and she figured the blinking mechanism had burned out. But since it still kept perfect time, she took it and hung it next to the door in her apartment.

"One of the first evenings after I handed over the keys to Russell's studio, I had a really bad night, missing him terribly, crying a lot, hardly sleeping. As I was leaving for work the next morning, those little lights started blinking. They blinked when I was leaving or when I came home." Eventually it stopped blinking and even though she put in new batteries, it hasn't blinked since.

The most mysterious and perhaps significant event she experienced in the aftermath of Russell's death involved a commemorative coin that fell off a shelf in her closet. It was inscribed with the phrase *Angel in my Pocket,* and Trudy had no idea where it had come from or how it had gotten into her closet. She put the coin on her key chain because it reminded her of Russell. A few weeks later, she woke up at two a.m. and couldn't get back to sleep. She turned on the TV and the movie *Angel in My Pocket* was on. She suddenly realized it was Russell's birthday. "He would have been sixty-seven and absolutely loved presents, even small ones." On that birthday, it seems he gave Trudy the most meaningful gift of all—a reminder of their years together and a nudge from the other side.

We come to know the unknowable through experiences like this, where awareness and intuition work together seamlessly to comfort and astonish us. We are left with a sense that death is simply a transition, a transformation of energy, and that our loved ones are always around, speaking softly. All we have to do is listen.

The Loon of Fourth Lake

When premonitions or visions have a correspondence in physical reality, Jung wrote, then it's a synchronistic phenomenon. And it's this type of synchronicity that Janice Cutbush experienced shortly after the sudden death of her husband, Tom.

She was visiting friends who live on the Fourth Lake in the Adirondacks in upstate New York. It was an area where she and Tom used to take their kids every summer when they were younger. Tom especially enjoyed listening to the loons on the lake early in the morning.

Late one afternoon, Janice went for a swim and suddenly felt a presence near her in the water. She looked up and saw an enormous loon about twenty feet away, all alone. He stayed nearby during her entire swim and left when she got out of the water. Every day of her visit, the loon appeared in front of her friend's home. They began calling him Tom. Her friend pointed out it was unusual to see a lone loon because they usually travel in pairs and mate for life.

Every year, Janice and her second husband vacation in the area, renting different homes on various lakes. "No matter where we are, our lone loon appears at some point during the vacation. I like to think it's Tom's spirit visiting us."

Janice's first experience might have gone unnoticed if she hadn't drawn the connection between Tom's love of loons and the loner who landed on the lake. Even though she wasn't asking specifically for spirit contact, Tom's death was still a raw wound and some part of her needed to know that his soul lived on. So her awareness and receptivity were factors in the experience.

This cluster of spirit contacts lasted for several years, whenever she visited the area. When you think about the oddity of the lone loon and the time period over which this contact lasted, it defies the odds.

Clusters of Dates & Numbers

You may see the same numbers on clocks, on cell phones, on microwaves, on the mileage counter at the gym, on price tags when you shop, on TV, on receipts. These numbers may recur with such frequency you might mention it to other people. If you do an Internet search for the numbers, perhaps you'll uncover their esoteric meanings or find websites where these numbers are discussed by others who have experienced them.

Jung experienced many numerical clusters through his life and came to believe that numbers represent "an archetype of order that has become conscious."[30] Their meaning may not be immediately apparent to you, so you'll have to dig around in your past and your own psyche to understand them. You might try meditating about them or incubating a dream or an experience that could illuminate the message for you. But other times, you get the message immediately.

Some of us might completely miss clusters of numbers that might hold importance in our lives, or maybe we do notice in passing and simply ignore.

Miriam was looking for a new job in the Internet technology field, and had two offers. The first one paid more and the job was located several minutes closer to her house than the second one. But she would be the only IT person working at the company. The second offer was much more interesting because she would work on a team and learn new skills. While she was deciding, she kept noticing the number two appearing over and over again, sometimes in multiples. She assumed it

---

30   Gerhard Adler and R.F.C. Hull. *The Structure and Dynamics of the Psyche* (*Collected Works of C.G. Jung, Volume 8*. New Jersey: Princeton University Press, 1970), 870.

didn't mean anything until several weeks later after she realized she'd made the wrong choice. She'd picked the first job, but soon realized she was isolated as the only IT person and the job was basic and boring. She wished she'd picked her number two choice.

Cardinals Everywhere

Sharon Catley of Vancouver recalls her father spent a great deal of time outdoors and when he became ill always pined for contact with nature. He especially missed watching birds and squirrels that came to feed in the backyard. One of Sharon's daughters installed a shelf near his bed and put three china birds on it and some birdseed in the middle of them. It looked as though they had landed and were about to feast. The brightest and most noticeable of the trio was a vibrant red cardinal. They remained with her father for years during his illness.

When he became too ill to remain at home, he was moved to a medical care facility and his birds accompanied him. At Christmas, a stained-glass art piece depicting several cardinals was hung in his window. The sun shining through them created a rosy glow. When Sharon's father died, her daughter salvaged the china birds and stained glass and saved them as a remembrance of her grandfather. The day he died, Sharon's mother was diagnosed with lung cancer.

Sharon was helping her mother clean up the basement of her house a few weeks after her father's death when she stepped on something sharp. Looking in the rug, she found a tiny piece of bright ruby red glass that could only have come from the stained-glass cardinals. That was the beginning of an astonishing array of appearances of cardinals in her life—something that connected directly to her father and convinced her he was in contact.

"I would open a magazine and there would be red cardinals. Looking around in a store or browsing a catalogue, I would see red cardinals adorning scarves, towels, cups, napkins, t-shirts, wall hangings, and dishes. Every one of them I saw reminded me of Dad. I just thought that maybe there had always been cardinals everywhere, but that I had never noticed them before or that they had somehow just become a popular decorating item."

It was not until the first Christmas after her dad's death that Sharon accepted the idea that the cardinals were being deliberately sent to her. "That year I received eleven Christmas cards. Seven of these had cardinals on them. I thought this must be a trend, that cardinals were in fashion that year." To test her theory, she examined Christmas cards at her place of work. "At Christmas, my company receives about two hundred cards and our secretary tapes them on the wall. I perused them, and there wasn't one cardinal on any of them."

A week later, Sharon was walking by the front desk when a receptionist was opening the morning mail. She called out to Sharon, "Come see how cute this card is." On her desk were a stack of late-arriving Christmas cards. The receptionist showed her a card with a snowy scene featuring a grove of birch trees. Nestled on a branch of one of the trees was a tiny cardinal.

Up to that point, Sharon had said nothing to anyone about her dad's gift of cardinals. But on her next trip to Calgary to visit her mother, now in failing health, she told her about the cardinals. She made a total of three trips that year to see her mother before she died.

On her last trip, a synchronicity would occur in a record shop that would lead to another incident of spirit contact. "While I was on my way home to Vancouver, I stopped at a Virgin Records store near my departure gate at the airport. While browsing the books, I noted that the last three songs playing on the store's intercom had all been older ones by Heart. I was thinking that there must be a new Heart Greatest Hits CD out."

However, when she looked in the CDs under *H*, she didn't find a single Heart album. She looked in the new releases, and didn't find Heart there, either. She quickly searched through the bargain bin, finally reaching deep and pulling out a CD whose label she couldn't see. To her surprise, it was Heart's *Greatest Hits*.

"When the cashier was ringing up my purchase, I told him about the synchronicity of finding the CD after hearing the music. He was surprised that they'd had the old CD in stock. He explained that the bosses weren't around so he'd decided to hook up his iPod to the intercom and listen to his own music."

Her mother died shortly afterward. Weeks later, while cleaning her house on Mother's Day, she had an urge to finally take out the Heart CD. For the first time, she examined the cover image. She knew it was a folk-art painting, but hadn't looked closely at it. The woman in the painting had red hair like her mother. She was holding open her sweater to reveal a bird cage within her torso and in the cage was a cardinal.

"To me, it means my mom and my dad are back together again and happy once more."

What's especially interesting about Sharon's clusters is that she immediately understood the connection between the cardinals and her dad. She was *aware*. She already believed that spirit contact was possible, so she didn't have to incubate anything, didn't struggle to interpret the clusters. She *knew*. She went about her life, aware and vigilant, and whenever a cardinal appeared in her experience, she accepted it as contact from her dad.

And that's really the way it should be with any spirit contact. While it's a fool's journey to dig around for possible connections, to see every little thing as spirit contact, to look for synchronicities where there aren't any, it's also unwise to overlook the obvious. By being dismissive, you miss out on the richness of connecting with loved ones who have passed.

PRACTICE 15: YOUR NUMBER CLUSTERS

Any time you experience a cluster of numbers or of numbers combined with other objects, like the lamp that blinked on three times on two successive nights for Anne, make note of it. If you're keeping a journal, jot down the details: date, time, your mood, your thoughts when the experience happened, and your interpretation. If you aren't sure what it means, note that, too.

For example, during a trip to Costa Rica several years ago, Trish went shopping for mementos to bring home. She was thinking about how her parents had raved about the country during a trip they'd made in the 1990s, and remembered her dad's descriptions of the dramatic countryside, the wildlife, the wonderful people. She and Megan nosed around in that shop for a long time and the bill was $111.11.

Eleven is the number Trish associates with spirit contact with her parents. She was so startled, she snapped a photo of the receipt. She wasn't sure what all those numbers meant, but it seemed to be about awareness. But awareness of what, she wondered. As she left the shop, Rob asked her if she had noticed the name of the shop. She looked up and smiled as she saw it was called Esperanza. That was the name of a novel she'd written that had been published a few months earlier. *Awareness*, she thought.

7

❋

How Altered States Help
You Connect with Spirit

WHEN THE SUBJECT of altered states of consciousness is mentioned, the first thing many people think about is drug-induced states of mind. While it's true that hallucinogenic drugs, in particular, can alter your consciousness and break through the veil between worlds, that's only one means of entering an altered state.

As a conduit to spirit contact, drugs present an array of issues. Besides the usual ones—legality, dangers of overdose, and bizarre behavior— there's also the question of whether or not such experiences are fantasies related to unconscious thoughts and attitudes, rather than actual spirit contact. So, we are not going to spend time in this chapter exploring drug use for spirit contact. However, ingesting drugs to contact the spirit world is an ancient practice of most primitive cultures, and we will touch on the subject again in chapter 9, Spirit of the Shamans.

Meditation is another method of reaching an altered state of consciousness and making contact with the other side, as the following story reveals.

One evening before a meditation class, Trish *asked* her deceased parents to communicate with her. She set an *intention*. And she *summoned strong desire* for this to occur. Midway through the meditation class, she opened her eyes and saw her parents in a corner of the room. They were laughing, vibrant, younger, and there was no evidence of the debilitating illnesses—Parkinson's and Alzheimer's—that had afflicted them in the last years of their lives. They were directing a group of people into a theater. When they realized she saw them, they faded away.

Spirit contact can be enhanced through deep relaxation, meditation, and other self-induced altered states of consciousness. Since meditation helps you to develop mindfulness—a purposeful awareness of yourself—it's easier to tap your intuition and connect with the spirit world than it is through your normal waking consciousness.

Of course, there are other reasons to meditate. Scientists have shown numerous health benefits that include lower blood pressure, heart rate, and cholesterol levels; reduced stress; and a slowing of the aging process. Meditation also decreases depression and moodiness, increases feelings of vitality and rejuvenation, and improves learning ability, memory, and emotional stability.

PRACTICE 16: ENTERING MEDITATION

Try these tips to begin or enhance a meditation practice, especially for the purpose of opening yourself to spirit contact and synchronicity.

Location

First, let's be clear that meditating anywhere is better than nowhere. That said, it's best to avoid places where you work, talk, or think a lot. Meditating at your desk in a home office or the kitchen table is probably not a good idea. If you're tired and meditate in bed, you'll probably drift off to sleep.

Sit on a comfortable chair or cushion. Some people meditate on their porch or in their garden. Others have a room in their home dedicated to meditation, set up with plants, fresh flowers, and perhaps a fountain or altar. Pick a time and place where you won't be disturbed. That might require closing a door and turning off your cell phone.

Invoke Protection

It's a good idea to protect yourself from any unwanted intrusions when seeking contact with the other side. Surround yourself from head to toe with a white or silver light or silvery protective garb. Invoke protection by saying: "Any contact I make with a spirit being will be benevolent and helpful. I am guided and protected."

Relax and Focus

That's not the definition of meditation, but it's the process. If you can relax and focus, you can meditate. If you've never meditated and think your mind never stops, start with a five-minute session. During that time, focus on your body. Notice how you feel and focus on your breath.

It probably won't be long before the internal chatter begins again, dragging you away from your present-moment awareness. You plan, reminisce, wonder, review, question, worry. You might think about what happened earlier or your plans for later. Just let it go.

Play with the idea of watching your thoughts, as if the real you is separate from them. In other words, be aware of your thoughts without getting caught up in them where one thought follows another and another. Return your focus to your breath or a single word or phrase, such as *one, love,* or *peace,* or *all is well, love life,* or *think nothing.*

Remain positive. Don't get frustrated if your thoughts continue to interfere with your meditation. You can gradually build toward twenty- to thirty-minute sessions. With practice, you'll reach a time and place beyond your thoughts ... and you might not want to leave!

If you're interested in contacting someone from the other side through meditation, here's a method for making contact.

State Your Intent

Have a specific target in mind, preferably someone you knew well. By the time you settle into place for your meditation, you should know whom you want to contact. If you have a photo of the person, place it in front of you. Take a few moments to think about your relationship with this person and your present feelings about the individual. Then, let go of your thoughts.

Breathe

As you quiet your mind, take several slow, deep breaths. Exhale fully, relaxing your belly. Inhale, holding the breath in your belly. Create warmth in your belly, expanding the area. Still holding your breath, relax into the feelings that surface. Let your body be sensitive and relaxed. Think of yourself becoming lighter and lighter. Hold your breath until it gets uncomfortable, then slowly exhale.

Focus on Your Body

Continue sitting quietly, letting the inner warmth rise and spread from your belly through your entire being. Imagine your cells, organs, tissues, muscles, and bones relaxing. Follow this movement down your legs to your toes, up your torso to your neck and head, down your arms to your fingertips. You can even bathe your thoughts in this warm, calm, relaxing sensation.

Making Contact

Concentrate lightly on your heart and focus on the image of the deceased loved one you want to reach. Let go of any feelings of guilt or sorrow you might feel regarding the person.

After a few moments, release all of it. Breathe gently, be alert for images, and listen for a voice that speaks to you.

If nothing happens or you're interrupted, realize that contact might come by another means, possibly through synchronicity—reading the person's name in the newspaper or on the Internet, hearing the name on the radio or television, or even seeing it on a street sign.

The next time you enter a meditative state, imagine a cord connecting you and the deceased loved one at the solar plexus. Maybe an image will come to mind or you'll hear a voice reassuring you, offering a message. Maybe nothing happens immediately, but after your session an object appears in an unusual place and you recognize it as a sign or symbol, a link to your departed loved one.

Alternately, as you move into a meditative state, picture blue sky from horizon to horizon, then imagine a tiny rectangular object at the zenith. You can project yourself upward to this object. You see that it's a platform, and you settle down on it. Relax and send out a message to the spirit you want to contact. The platform is your place of connection. You might even find the spirit of your loved one waiting for you. You can visit at any time and from the platform you can leap off into other worlds, other dimensions.

A Healing Visit

Another method of entering an altered state is through a session with a Reiki healer. Reiki is a healing technique from Japan that alleviates stress and promotes relaxation. Practitioners move their hands just above a person's body. The intent is to connect with *ki*, the life force energy recognized by Eastern philosophies.

One day, Connie Cannon, a retired nurse who lives in Florida, had a Reiki healing with a friend, Jenny. While on the table, Connie silently asked for her father to be with her, if he possibly could. She didn't mention this to her friend.

During her healing session, Connie saw her dad standing at the end of the table, his hands on her feet. He was wearing his usual work attire that she remembered—khakis and a plaid flannel shirt. "The energy in the room was so electric that the room literally seemed to hum." Neither one spoke during the session.

A few moments after the healing, Connie asked Jenny if she would write down everything she'd experienced. Connie said she would do the same and they would compare notes. Jenny began by describing the presence of a healing spirit, a young-looking man with warm brown eyes and thick, dark auburn hair, who was wearing a Masonic ring on the ring finger of his right hand. She wrote that he was wearing khakis and Western boots.

"My dad died at age forty-two. He was a 33rd-degree Mason and wore his ring on his right hand. He had brown eyes and auburn hair, and was a cattleman who went to work in khakis and western boots. I knew he was with us."

Jenny went on to say the man had assisted in the healing, and stood at the end of table. She said he kept the energy flow closed within her energy field. Jenny also said she heard a high frequency in the room and felt as if she were in a trance and that a current was racing through her during the healing.

When Connie got in her car to drive home, she turned on the radio. It was silent for a couple of seconds, then an old song by Eddie Fisher, "Oh My Papa," came on and filled the car with beautiful, comforting words. "I laughed and cried, knowing my dad was right there. That was no coincidence."

Out-of-Body Experience

Maybe you've had a dream in which you hovered near the ceiling in a second body and stared down at your sleeping body. Or perhaps you soared away to explore the neighborhood or distant places or even other realms of reality. These out-of-body experiences (OBEs) probably happen spontaneously more often than we realize, but we don't always remember them.

"It turns out that solid scientific evidence reveals that millions of Americans have had an out-of-body experience," writes Dr. Kevin Nelson, a professor of neurology at the University of Kentucky, in an article called "Are Out-of-Body Experiences Always Spiritual?" in *Psychology Today*.[31] "It's probably safe to say that many consider these experiences evidence that an afterlife exists and that our consciousness or soul can separate from our body."

If OBEs are actual journeys, as experiencers purport, and not fantasies, then the answer to Dr. Nelson's question is a resounding yes. After all, if you are out of body, you are a spirit! And many out-of-body travelers report contact with spirit beings.

Journeys Out of the Body, by Robert Monroe, is a classic tome on the subject. Monroe was a Virginia businessman who recorded his fantastic journeys over the course of three decades. His early experiences occurred spontaneously and he had no idea what was happening to him. He would lie down to go to sleep and within minutes his body would start to shudder violently, and he would feel as if he couldn't move. It took all of his willpower to force himself to sit up and come fully awake. After several such experiences, he thought there was something physically wrong, like epilepsy or a brain tumor. However, his family doctor said he was in perfect health.

That was when Monroe decided to explore the sensation, which continued to occur over the next few months. One night when the vibrations started, Monroe realized he could move his fingers. His arm was hanging over the side of the bed and his fingers were touching the rug. So he pressed down with his fingers, and they seemed to penetrate the rug. He pushed harder and his hand sank into the floor.

He went back to his doctor, who advised him to lose some weight, smoke less, and to look into yoga—an odd suggestion for a doctor to make in the 1950s. Some yoga practitioners, the doctor explained, claimed they could travel out of their bodies at will. The vibrations came

---

31   Kevin Nelson, MD. "Are Out-of-Body Experiences Always Spiritual?" *Psychology Today*, November 3, 2010. https://www.psychologytoday .com/blog/the-spiritual-doorway-in-the-brain/201011/are-out -body-experiences-always-spiritual.

and went six more times before Monroe gathered the nerve to explore out-of-body travel. Finally, one night when the vibrations came in full force, he thought of floating upward—and did.

That was the beginning of his experiences, which included journeys to the past, the future, and to other dimensions—including the afterlife, journeys that are sometimes referred to as *astral travel*. In the late 1970s, Monroe opened the Monroe Institute for students and researchers to explore and study out-of-body travel, the nature of consciousness, and spirit contact.

Another adventurer journeyed to a place he had heard where knowledge and the events of our lives are stored. In esoteric literature, that place is known as the Akashic Record. When he arrived, he found someone waiting for him.

Wesley Meeks has traveled out of body since he was twelve. The experiences began spontaneously, and eventually he learned how to initiate and direct his OBEs. Now in his mid-fifties, Meeks has accumulated more than four decades of journeys that have taken him everywhere from a nightclub to realms beyond space and time. The latter are sometimes referred to as *astral planes*, hence the term *astral travel*, which is often used interchangeably with out-of-body travel.

Such extraordinary experiences might seem surprising when you consider Meeks's career in law enforcement and security. He spent fifteen years as a police officer in west Texas, where he still lives. Then he worked another eight years as a child welfare investigator, and three years as a private detective. He now supervises surveillance operations at a hospital. As you might imagine, he doesn't talk much with his associates or friends about his OBEs. However, since 2015 he has related many of his experiences to us through e-mails, some of which have appeared on our blog. This particular journey took place in 2005 or 2006, Meeks said.

"I had gone to bed and before getting sleepy, I told myself that I intended to have an out-of-body experience and that I wanted to go to a place I had heard about. I did not really know what the place was called, but I had read books about OBEs, and some writers told of a huge mansion where all souls live when they are between lives. It's a place where knowledge and the events of our lives are stored."

As he began to get drowsy, Wesley relaxed his entire body. He focused on his target, slowed his breath, and began counting backwards from nine hundred. "As was usual for me, a ringing starting in my head and my body vibrated from head to toe. I felt my body getting heavier and heavier. That's when I mentally pushed, and I was out of my body." He pointed out that he was relaxed, but still awake. "Next I shot through the ceiling and up into the night sky. For the first few minutes, the experience of free flight was so exhilarating that I temporarily lost sight of my mission.

"If you have ever seen the beginning of the Star Trek shows where the Enterprise suddenly goes into warp speed and the stars begin to flash by at hundreds per second, this is sort of the same sensation I have when I fly through the night sky. It is such a sensation of freedom, and I suspect it is the same sensation that people feel when they leave the body permanently."

After a few minutes, he focused on his predetermined mission. "As soon as I thought about my target, I was no longer flying at warp speed. Now I was floating gently toward an enormous mansion. I floated above it and just watched for a while. There is no way I can even begin to describe the beauty of this mansion, the ornateness, the intricateness of the design and details. I cannot even guess at its size. As I floated there, I saw that there were other people floating, some entering smaller compartments in the enormous mansion, some leaving the mansion. Some were visible as people, but others were auras of different colors. Yet, somehow I knew they were people."

Wesley estimated the rooms in the mansion as about the size of a large hotel room, but instead of furniture, each one contained a single large vase about two or three times the size of a human body. "The vases were beautiful beyond description and each one was unique. Some appeared to be of marble, some of granite, some of jade, and others of materials I could not name. There were designs and inscriptions on each vase. The mansion itself was so pure white that it was brilliant, but the floors of each of the compartments were of a material like marble, and so smooth they shone like glass."

He noted the compartments had three walls with the fourth side opening into the courtyard. "I saw people walking around on the broad sidewalk and sitting in very ornately designed benches. There was a swimming pool in the center of the courtyard, and there was a fountain that was about ten feet taller than the edge of the pool, and from this fountain a gentle waterfall flowed constantly into the pool."

While he was viewing the mansion in utter amazement, an older woman approached him. Wesley, who was in his forties at the time, thought this woman was in her sixties. "She was very regal and attractive and was wearing a flowing gown. She asked me if I knew what I was looking at, and I said I wasn't sure. The woman told me to come sit with her on a bench.

"We floated downward and landed on the sidewalk, then walked a short distance to a very beautiful bench. We sat down and the woman explained to me that the mansion was built by the Creator and it was so large that I could not see all of it at once. She explained that each soul had a room in the mansion, and pointed toward one of the rooms.

"She told me that the large vase in the room contained all the knowledge that the soul had gained while going through various lives on the earth and in other places as well. She did not explain the 'other places' and I was too overwhelmed to ask her. The woman told me that people lived many lives, as well as spent time between lives by staying on different planes that are not visible to humans on the physical realm."

Then the woman said something that puzzled him. "She said that people in the astral realms sometimes disguised themselves for various reasons while they traveled. Sometimes people did not want to be recognized, or needed to appear differently for other reasons. Sometimes they didn't use bodies at all, but moved around as auras. She also said that people could appear older or younger than they really were on the physical plane, or even be of a different race than in the physical plane.

"Then she told me that she was not actually an older woman, but was really my age. She said that she travelled as an older woman both to appear wiser and trustworthy to new travelers, and so that some people would not recognize her."

Wesley was still baffled by the covert aspects of astral travel. Next the woman stood up from the bench and instantly was a fairly attractive female of about forty to forty-five years old. Her clothing suddenly vanished and she was nude. Interestingly, the first thing he noticed was that she had a green aura surrounding her body.

"I sensed that she wanted to have a sexual encounter with me. Then she said aloud that she wanted to make love, if I wanted to. I realized I was nude at this point, and actually I am not sure that I have ever even thought about clothing while I traveled. But I was suddenly overcome with both an erotic feeling and the realization that I desired to bond with her. But I remember thinking that all these other people were around and were watching. She told me to look around, and I noticed that many people were engaged in what appeared to be sexual contact all over the courtyard as well as while floating above it! I realized now that both of us were floating and that I also had an aura that I think was blue. She moved towards me and I embraced her."

Wesley went on to describe his sexual encounter with the woman. "Our auras merged and we merged too. *Merge* is the best word I can think of, because we were two, but we were literally *one* at the same time… We were joined in soul and mind. I cannot even begin to describe the total pleasure, the total ecstasy. It was the greatest pleasurable feeling I have ever had in my life. We were two parts of one creation. It was like a huge electrical shock, like being struck by lightning for several minutes, but not at all painful."

When it was over, the woman instantly assumed the form of the older persona, and advised him to return to his body. "She told me there was so much for me to learn and that she hoped she would see me again sometime, then disappeared. I suddenly felt sucked back into my body and I was instantly lying in bed awake. I was tingling and vibrating all over. I literally could not move, and I was tired, but exhilarated at the same time. The tingling was so severe that the bed was shaking and I actually thought that I would wake my wife. But this tingling sensation eventually subsided to a dull tingle, but lasted for three days after the experience."

If you're able to remember a spontaneous OBE, you might be motivated to learn techniques for out-of-body travel so you can consciously direct your journeys. You might visit a friend's house, where you spot something new or unusual, such as an object on a shelf. Later, you can inquire about what you saw and find out if it's an actual physical object. That would provide evidence that you actually traveled out of body and didn't just dream that you did.

With experience, you can journey far from your home or neighborhood. You can pierce the veil between worlds and contact a departed loved one or a spirit guide.

Practice 17: How to Enter an OBE

Over the years of Robert Monroe's experiences in out-of-body travel, he developed a technique for leaving his body that he wrote about in his first book, *Journeys Out of the Body*. The method we prescribe here is adapted from his book. [32]

Protection

Since fear is one of the primary hindrances to out-of-body travel, it's a good idea to invoke protection before launching an out-of-body journey. At the Monroe Institute, a prayer of protection is used:

> I deeply desire the help and cooperation, the assistance, and understanding of those individuals whose wisdom, development and experience are equal or greater than my own. I request their guidance and protection from any influence or any source that might provide me with less than my stated desires.

Invoking protection not only provides an actual safeguard, but it can help you quickly move ahead on your journey by allowing you to eliminate your fears. It also becomes part of your ritual for entering an OBE. As such, the prayer serves as a trigger. In other words, it signals your body you're about to embark on another journey. You're safe and ready to go.

Relaxation

Look over the relaxation techniques described earlier in the chapter. Your goal is to reach that drowsy state between wakefulness and sleep and to maintain it without falling asleep. Set your intention, but don't analyze. Focus and relax. As you become relaxed and start to drift off, hold your mental attention on something—an idea, an object, even an emotion—with your eyes closed. Once you can hold that borderland state indefinitely without falling asleep, you've passed the first stage.

---

32   Robert Monroe. *Journeys Out of the Body: The Classic Work on Out-of-Body Experience.* (New York: Doubleday, 1971).

The second stage of relaxation is to maintain the border and state without concentrating on anything. Just focus on the blackness in front of you. Let go of any anxiety. The third stage involves releasing any rigid hold on the borderland sleep and drifting deeper into your conscious mind.

Creating the Vibrations

The vibrational field that is essential to entering an OBE seems easiest to create if your head is positioned in the direction of magnetic north, according to Monroe. Make sure your room isn't completely dark so that you have some light for a point of reference. Maintain your conscious awareness, but relax as deeply as you can. Then give yourself the suggestion that you'll recall everything you experience that is beneficial to your physical and mental well-being. Repeat the suggestion a few times to reinforce it.

To set up the vibrational waves, imagine two lines extending from the sides of your head and converging about a foot in front of your eyes. Think of these lines as charged wires that are joined, or as poles of a magnet that are connected. Once they converge, extend them three feet from your forehead, and then six feet. Now you must move the intersected lines ninety degrees until they are directly over your head. Then reach out toward the point of intersection through the top of your head.

Keep reaching until you feel a reaction. It may feel like a surging, hissing, rhythmically pulsating wave that roars into your head; let it sweep through your entire body. At this point, your body may become rigid and immobile.

Controlling the Vibrations

Once the vibrations start, you need to eliminate the fear and panic you might experience. The first time you encounter the vibrations, you might feel like you're being electrocuted, even though there is no pain. To end the session, simply lie quietly and analyze what's taking place until the vibrations fade away on their own.

When you're familiar with the sensation and have moved beyond fear, you're ready to control the vibrations. Mentally direct them into a ring that sweeps around your body, moving from head to toe and back again. Once you've got the momentum going, let it proceed on its own. The faster the vibrations, the easier it is to disassociate yourself from the physical.

It takes practice to smooth out the vibrations. But eventually, you should be able to start the vibrations simply on a mental command, thus eliminating some of the earlier steps.

Thought Control

Focus on a single thought, such as *float upward* or *up and out*. At this point, your thought should instantly translate into action. However, the fear factor might be triggered again. That will bring you back to a familiar place—your body.

Separation and Lifting Out

On your first attempt, you might just separate your hand and explore the area immediately around you. Find an object, maybe something on a bed stand. See if you can identify it by touch.

Once you're comfortable with this partial disassociation, the easiest way to fully separate from your body is to imagine yourself lifting out and floating upward. Feel yourself getting lighter and lighter and think about how pleasurable it will be to float free. If you can maintain these thoughts, you'll lift out easily. Or you can turn on your side and rotate your way out, as if you're slowly turning over in your bed.

When you're out, you can explore your immediate area. If you want to go farther, simply think about where you want to go. The clearer your request, the faster you move ahead to your target.

If you want to travel to the spirit world, focus on an individual, preferably a deceased friend or family member, and request contact. Since you are going out of body, you are traveling to the spirit world, rather than a spirit visiting you in the borderland of this world.

Between Dimensions

Connie, who provided a spirit contact story earlier in this chapter, recalled an experience she initially thought was a lucid dream, in which she had contact with her dad. In retrospect, though, she believes it was an out-of-body experience.

"I found myself sitting in a straight-backed chair on this side of what appeared to be an enormous frame, like an unadorned picture frame. The only other thing in this space was a chair matching mine on the other side of the frame."

As she watched and waited for something to happen, her father moved into the empty space on the other side of the frame and walked toward her. "I said, 'Oh, Daddy, it's really you.' I started to stand up to hug him, but he put his hand out to stop me. He said, 'Honey, you can't touch me. I'm with you, but your space is not my space.'"

He sat down and told her that he was coming to get her. "I wasn't frightened in the least and asked, 'Soon?' He replied, 'Yes.' We were silent for a minute or so, then I asked him, 'Daddy, is it beautiful there?' Suddenly he became pure blinding radiance. It lasted a mere second or two, and then he was himself again, as I remembered him. Then, with the most radiant smile he told me, 'Honey, it's so beautiful!' After a few more moments, the scene vanished and I was back in my body. I opened my eyes, wanting terribly to go back there."

But the contact wasn't quite over. "I was aware for maybe a minute of the odor of cigarettes. Dad smoked Lucky Strikes. Then I was totally immersed by the fragrance of Old Spice, which Dad always wore. There is not a smidgen of doubt in my mind that my dad and I were together, just in some type of spatial separation, yet able to communicate."

For Connie, the experience was proof that we continue to exist after we leave our human bodies and that there are numerous dimensions where our spirits may go when we leave.

Near-Death Experiences

Short of the ultimate journey, there is no deeper altered state of consciousness than the one known as near-death experience (NDE). While many consciousness researchers willingly explore out-of-body experiences, NDEs are another matter. No one, other than the characters in the movie *Flatliners,* chooses to die for the experience, and then hopefully come back. Most NDEs take place in the presence of medical personnel who are frantically trying to save the person's life.

Thanks to the curiosity of medical researchers, extensive research exists about people who have had near-death experiences, often during surgery, and are subsequently revived. When they return to full consciousness, many of them remember the experience and recount how they met dead family members and relatives or evolved spiritual beings. They're often convinced their experiences were real. The International Association for Near Death Studies describes elements of NDEs this way: "An NDE typically includes one or more of the following: a sense of leaving the body; movement, often through a tunnel; being engulfed in light or darkness; feelings of intense and indescribable love, peace and sometimes terror; perceived encounters with deceased loved ones, unfamiliar entities and/or spiritual presences; a life review; a landscape; an overpowering sense of knowledge and purpose. The effects of an NDE or related experience are often powerful, enduring, and may be life-altering."[33]

Raymond Moody was one of the first physicians to research the survival of consciousness after death. In his 1975 book, *Life After Life,* he

---

33   International Association for Near Death Studies, Inc. "What is a Near-Death Experience?" http://iands.org/about/about-iands27/press-releases.html.

coined the term "near-death experience" and mapped out the topography of these experiences. Since then, others have delved into this study of consciousness and added to the growing knowledge.

Laurin Bellg, a critical care doctor, interviewed fifty patients who had near-death experiences for her book, *Near Death in the ICU*. They described astonishing encounters with lost loved ones, felt intense love and peace, and had extreme reluctance to return to their physical lives. Skeptics contend that people who have NDEs already believed in such experiences so they were predisposed to have them. But Bellg disagrees. "In fact, one patient who shared his near-death encounter with me was an atheist, believed nothing existed beyond the physical, and had his world view turned upside down by what had happened to him." [34]

Many who have NDEs recall hovering several feet above their bodies while watching the frantic activity below them. Vicki DeLaurentis drowned at the age of sixteen. She recalls drifting upward and seeing a body on the beach as CPR was administered. A wonderful feeling of peace and warmth spread through her. Someone behind her kept asking her different questions, and then the voice told her to look more closely at the girl on the beach. "I slowly realized she looked like me—and then BAM! I was on the beach looking up at the sky." Water gushed out of her nose, ears, and eyes. The paramedics clamped an oxygen mask on her. "One reason why I personally feel it was real and not a hallucination is that I still remember it like it just happened—that was four decades ago."

For years, Eben Alexander was a neurosurgeon and physician who had refused to believe that consciousness survived death. Despite anecdotes by thousands of people who have experienced NDEs, Alexander couldn't reconcile the evidence with his scientific training. Then his brain was attacked by a rare illness that plunged him into a coma for a week. He was hooked up to life support and essentially brain dead.

---

34   Laurin Bellg, MD. *Near Death in the ICU*. (Cornwall-on-Hudson: Sloan Publishing, 2015), 75.

Doctors advised his family to turn off the life support systems and as this option was being considered, Alexander awakened. His 2012 memoir, *Proof of Heaven*, recounts his experiences in that netherworld of "brain dead." He met an angelic being who guided him into a realm where he met and spoke with "the Divine source of the universe itself." He wrote: "Communicating with God is the most extraordinary experience imaginable, yet at the same time it's the most natural one of all, because God is present in all of us." [35]

What makes Alexander's book a big deal is that not only was he a neurosurgeon, but also a self-avowed disbeliever. He and Moody and a handful of others have bolstered the case for the survival of consciousness after death in much the same way that psychiatrist Brian Weiss did for reincarnation when he wrote *Many Lives, Many Masters*.

Lost Love

Some stories about spirit communication whisk us into realms we may find unbelievable. Is it possible for both an out-of-body experiencer and a spirit to manifest as completely physical beings in a nonordinary realm?

Liz grew up in a small town in North Carolina. As a young woman, she became close to her physician, Dr. George W. He became her confidante, and even though he was married, she suspected he'd fallen in love with her. When she decided to marry a local man, George begged her not to do it, that she was making the wrong choice. After Liz and Darrell married, they moved to Nebraska and she lost touch with George. Later, she understood George's concern about her husband, who became involved with another woman. In spite of his behavior, she stayed with him and they raised three children.

Liz never forgot about George, but he definitely wasn't on her mind the night in 2015 when she dreamed of him. In the dream, he told her

---

35   Eben Alexander. *Proof of Heaven: A Neurosurgeon's Journey into the Afterlife.* (New York: Simon & Schuster, 2012), 161.

that he'd died. Later, she verified he'd died two years earlier. After that, he was often on her mind.

Liz meditates regularly, and even has a designated room for her practice. One day during meditation, she spontaneously projected out of her body and found herself with George. "There was nothing else, no environment, nothing around us, just empty space, and we were standing against each other like a couple slow-dancing. He was as corporeal, as tangible, as three-dimensional as I was."

She was sure it wasn't a dream or her imagination. "As we stood there, body against body, we melded into one entity, the intensity so exquisite that it eludes description. It was beyond sensual or sexual sensations. We literally became one, an undulating column of blinding electric blue light that transcends. The experience lasted perhaps two minutes. Nothing was spoken. There was no sound. Then, George was gone and I was back in my room alone... more alone than I have ever been."

She said the experience left her with more questions than answers "about the nature of reality, the nature of time, the nature of Being." She went on to say: "Now I have the conviction that there is some dimension, some space, some place, where the deceased are able to be once again physical, at least momentarily... and can be touched."

PRACTICE 18: VISUALIZING CONTACT

To make contact with a lost loved one, first set your intention. Who would you like to encounter among loved ones who have passed over? Imagine what the person looks like. Maybe you have a picture that you can use as a reminder.

When you're ready to proceed, move into a relaxed, meditative state by following the recommendations in the earlier practice. Once you are settled down and have let go of all distracting thoughts, imagine you are walking along a trail through a wooded landscape. The trail gradually curves and you come upon a grassy field. You can see cows in the distance and hear bells on their necks clanging like wind chimes.

You raise your gaze and see a hot air balloon slowly descending onto the field. Notice its color, and whether the color is solid or striped. As you move toward it, focus on the carriage that is now landing on the field. You can see someone inside and as you move closer, you realize it's the one you're hoping to contact.

At this point, you may think that it's all your imagination. But realize that something more may also be involved. You might take a few more full breaths to move you into a deeper altered state. It's time to watch and listen with your inner vision and hearing. Maybe other senses come into play. Take your time. See what happens.

Don't be disappointed if the connection seems vague or nonexistent. The hot air balloon can return during another session. With intent and practice, you'll make contact.

8

❋

Contact in
Your Dreams

DREAMS, THOSE NIGHTTIME forays into fantastical realms, are probably the most common venues spirits use to speak to us. Our conscious minds are the quietest and we are more likely to accept the experience as something meaningful. Some of the most profound and vivid dreams that connect us to the other side are those that occur near the time of death of a loved one, or shortly afterward.

Such dreams are often startling, powerful, and unexpected. Their vibrancy and intensity distinguish them from normal dreams. When Rob's cousin John appeared to him in a vivid dream, he resonated health and vigor. But he seemed a bit confused, and asked, "What's going on?" At the time of the dream, John was in a coma. He died a day later.

Rob wasn't close to his cousin and had only seen him once—at the funeral for Rob's father—since they were kids. He'd heard that John was ill, but wasn't thinking about him before the dream. That raises the question of why John would appear to Rob, who was clearly a distant relation. Was it because Rob was open to such phenomenon and somehow accessible? Or was it because the distance between them made it easier to connect with Rob than with grieving family members? As a result, he contacted John's survivors, expressed condolences, and related the dream. In a sense, he had acted as an intermediary, and honored the dream by reporting the contact. It's always a good idea to follow through on any message or wishes you might receive from a departed loved one. That could involve anything from forwarding a message to someone to completing a task left undone by the deceased.

Trish's eighty-four-year-old mother died from complications from Alzheimer's in 2000 and five years later, her father, ninety-two, died from complications from Parkinson's. Over the years, she had a series of dreams about her parents that seemed to be direct communication from them, allowing her to track their progress through the afterlife. Many of these dreams were incubated, where she specifically asked for contact with her parents.

In the early dreams, when her father was still alive, Trish would see her mother pushing her walker down a corridor in the Alzheimer's unit where she'd spent the last two years of her life. She was crying, confused about where she was, and kept calling out for her husband. Then, not long before Trish's father passed away, she dreamed that her mother was no longer using a walker, looked younger and more vibrant, and was playing bridge with friends, just as she used to when she was alive. Trish took this as a positive sign that her mother had recovered from the Alzheimer's she'd suffered from the last six or seven years of her life.

Not long after her father passed away, she dreamed that her parents were throwing a party and a number of their dead brothers and sisters were in attendance. They both looked to be in their late thirties or early forties, and in the dream, her father assured Trish they were fine.

PRACTICE 19: IDENTIFYING CONTACT DREAMS

If you've never had a dream of contact with the other side, you might wonder what the difference is between a true dream of spirit contact and an ordinary dream about a departed loved one. Here are some common themes of visitation dreams.

- The dream is vivid and feels real. Colors are often dynamic, and objects and scenery are sharp and clear.

- The dead person seems very much alive, and healthy. The spirit's energy level is dynamic, positive, and uplifting.

- You sense without a doubt the contact is real and it's not an ordinary dream.

- The dream sticks with you throughout the day and beyond. You have no trouble remembering it.

- Messages are often brief and to the point. The most common missive is that the deceased is doing fine now and not to worry. If trouble is on your horizon, you might get a warning message. But it will probably be delivered in a kind and loving manner.

- When you wake up, you might feel cheered and revitalized, and carry a sense of warmth and wonder into your day.

PRACTICE 20: HOW TO INITIATE CONTACT

If you would like to make use of the dream state to reconnect with a departed loved one, or encounter a spirit guide, how do you go about it? Can you program such a dream?

- As with all forms of contact with the other side, you need to recognize you have a natural ability to pierce the veil between worlds. In doing so, your awareness expands.

- Set your specific intention. Do you want to contact a deceased friend or family member? Are you seeking guidance from an enlightened being?

- Once you set that intention, make sure you have a specific reason for making contact beyond simple curiosity. What do you want to know? If you just want confirmation that the person is okay, then make that your stated reason.

- When you're ready for bed, invoke protection by saying any contact you make with a spirit being will be benevolent and helpful. Imagine your body surrounded by a white or silver light. Or you might imagine yourself wearing a silvery form-fitting protective outfit that covers you head to toe.

- Make sure you have pen and paper or a recording device at your bedside so you can spell out everything that happened while it's still fresh in your mind.

- Now you're ready to *incubate* your dream. Before going to sleep, repeat your intention, and stoke it with desire. Ask your question or state your specific desire. Know that you'll make contact, and when you do, you'll remember everything that occurs in your dream.

Healing Dream Contact

Connie's dream request was for healing and was specific. She had accidentally hit one of her front lower teeth with a hairbrush and loosened it. The tooth was painful for several days and moved every time she ate or spoke. Finally, one night while lying in bed in excruciating pain, she decided to call on a dentist in spirit for help. Dr. S was a man she had known well years earlier.

"That night I called on the spirit of Dr. S, and asked if he could please come and help me. I dreamed about him, and in the dream he was pulling that tooth. About 3 a.m., I woke up and noticed the tooth wasn't hurting. I put my finger in my mouth and didn't feel the tooth. I discovered it had been pulled and was lying in the front of my mouth."

Connie said there was no pain whatsoever. She took the tooth out, set it on the bedside table, then got up to check for bleeding. She was shocked to discover the entire tooth, root and all, had been removed. There wasn't a single drop of blood. She didn't have any doubt that Dr. S had actually pulled the tooth and then had awakened her so she wouldn't swallow it.

She noted that front teeth have very deeply embedded roots and are difficult to extract. "But Dr. S has enormous energy. Grateful doesn't even begin to express my feelings. What a gift of healing from a loving spirit."

Not everyone has such dramatic encounters with spirits, of course, especially on first attempts. If you don't make contact on your initial effort, keep at it. It could be the spirit is right there, but you're not yet ready for what the contact will entail. It also could be that your spirit guide was calling to you in your dreams before you began seeking that contact. In other words, your awareness, intention, and desire were triggered by a nudge from the other side to prepare you for the contact.

When you do make contact with a departed loved one, the spirit might appear to you in a revived form, healthier in appearance and years younger than at the time of death. That appearance can be comforting for the seeker and reflect the revived spirit's awareness in the afterlife. Alternately, you might glimpse a spirit in the form of a glowing ball of light. In spite of that appearance, chances are you'll intuitively recognize the luminous form as the spirit of a loved one.

In the aftermath of the death of Rob's father, Don, his mother saw her late husband in both forms. One day, while doing laundry in the basement, a globe of light appeared in the doorway for several seconds and she sensed it was Don visiting in spirit. But on a couple of occasions, she saw him in physical form. The most memorable was an appearance in the den where she was resting on a comfortable chair. "I opened my eyes and there he was, wearing an orange patterned shirt that I'd never seen. I said, 'Where did you get that shirt?' He smiled and faded away."

It's as if spirits have access to a cosmic wardrobe where they can alter their appearance in ways that will grab your attention in your dreams and visions. The same is true for spirit guides who might appear in your dreams playing the role of ordinary people, such as a bus driver, a ticket taker, a friendly fellow passenger, or a tour guide. But their interactions with you offer a hint at their true role as a guide from the other side.

Lucid Dreams

Once you're proficient at remembering and interpreting your dreams and even incubating them, you can pursue lucid dreaming, a higher level of dream work. It's when you are consciously aware that you're dreaming and able to affect events within the dream. Awakening inside a dream is a momentous accomplishment, whether it happens spontaneously or through a concerted effort on your part.

The sensation is extremely exhilarating and memorable, even if the experience only lasts a few seconds. In the lucid state, you can do things that defy normal reality. You can fly, walk through a wall, or dance on the ceiling. You can consciously attempt to make contact with a departed loved one, or the spirits themselves might trigger the lucid awareness. Most people spontaneously experience their first lucid dream before they become interested in learning the steps to generate a lucid dream. The surprising and usually joyous experience of dream flying, in fact, might trigger your lucid dreaming experience. So might a frightening nightmare. Regardless, entering a lucid dream isn't easy and often takes persistence. Here are hints to help you become a lucid dreamer that were adapted from techniques described by Stephen LaBerge in *Lucid Dreaming: The Power of Being Awake & Aware in Your Dreams*.[36] LaBerge noted that he adapted his techniques from German gestalt psychologist Paul Tholey.

---

36   Stephen LaBerge. *Lucid Dreaming: The Power of Being Awake & Aware in Your Dreams.* (New York: Ballantine, 1985), 138-166.

PRACTICE 21: TECHNIQUE TO ENTER A LUCID DREAM

1. Ask yourself repeatedly during the day, "Am I dreaming?" By doing so and questioning your state of consciousness, you will train your unconscious mind to do the same at night while you are dreaming. Another similar cueing method, recommended by Andrew Holecek, author of *Dream Yoga: Illuminating Your Life Through Lucid Dreaming and the Tibetan Yogas of Sleep*[37], is jump up and down from time to time during the day. When your dream body does the same thing, you might keep going up or drop back down and sink or float into the ground. It's a great way of recognizing that you're dreaming.

2. Before going to bed, set a strong intention to remember your dreams and that when you're dreaming, you'll become consciously aware that you are doing so. Tell yourself that any unusual images or sensations, such as footprints on the ceiling, someone walking by with a fifteen-foot-long carrot, or your ability to fly or float will trigger your awareness that you're dreaming. You might awaken within a dream when you hear powerful, inspiring music or simply a voice whispering in your ear, telling you to look around. That could be a call from the other side, and a chance to make contact with a departed loved one or spirit guide.

3. You might find an opportunity to enter a lucid dream just as you are starting to fall asleep. As you get drowsy and drift into the first state of sleep, you'll see a rapid series of hypnogogic images flashing in front of your mind's eye. In this state of light sleep, you are still awake. But you must remain so in order to experience a lucid dream.

---

37 Andrew Holecek. *Dream Yoga: Illuminating Your Life Through Lucid Dreaming and the Tibetan Yogas of Sleep*. (Boulder, CO: Sounds True, 2016), 46.

4. Don't be upset if you don't immediately become lucid. Pay attention to any dreams you had, especially early in the morning. Think about the details and go over the dream a few times. Jot down the highlights so you don't forget. You can rewrite and expand later. Did you experience any unusual or impossible abilities, such as walking through walls or flying? Did dream characters shape-shift into different people or animals? Did you see anything that would be impossible in the everyday world? Did you experience strong emotions or intense sensations, such as cosmic music or expanded vision?

5. Go back to sleep in the same position and focus on reentering the dream. Again, tell yourself: *One, I'm dreaming… two, I'm dreaming.* And on and on. At some point, as you repeat the phrase, you will be dreaming. As images come to you, look for a dream sign. Then think of something you might want to do in this dream. Perhaps you might call on someone from the spirit world.

This Man

While most dream contact with the other side involves interactions with deceased loved ones or spirit guides, there is considerable evidence that certain entities from the spirit world haunt the dreams of many people. It's worthwhile to take a look at this mysterious and intrusive side of contact, since it might be the only form of spirit communication that many people experience. First, there's the curious case of a being often referred to as *This Man*.

In January 2001, the patient of a well-known New York psychiatrist drew the face of a man who repeatedly appeared in her dreams. The drawing revealed a man with a round face, heavy eyebrows, dark eyes, a thin upper lip, and a receding hairline. In some instances, the man gave her advice on her personal life. The woman said she had never met the man in her daily life. Only in her dreams.

The drawing remained on the therapist's desk for a few days until another patient spotted it and recognized the face. He said the man had often visited him in his dreams and that in his waking life, he'd never met the man. [38]

The psychiatrist decided to send the portrait to a few of his colleagues who have patients with repetitive dreams. Within a few months, four patients recognized the man as a recurring presence in their dreams. All of the patients referred to him as *This Man.*

In the ten years since the original portrait was drawn, more than two thousand people worldwide have claimed they've seen This Man in their dreams. Most of the dreamers consider the man benevolent, and many say he helps them escape from their dreams. Some call him romantic; others fly with him in their dreams. Some consider him a guide.

Hat Man

Another dream figure, Hat Man, has been seen by far more people. Rather than benevolent, he usually incites terror in dreamers that blends momentarily into their waking life. Typically, the Hat Man is a shadowy figure with no visible facial features who appears after dark. No eyes or nose or chin are visible, and his body is usually draped in a cape or a trench coat, which blends in with the surrounding darkness. He is best known for his wide-brimmed hat, and his ominous and threatening demeanor.

So many people have had dream-nightmare encounters with this entity that Heidi Hollis wrote a book, *The Hat Man: The True Story of Evil Encounters.*[39] The book is filled with nightmarish encounters that occur in the early morning hours. Without exception, these encounters are negative. No one enjoys the unexpected company of the Hat

---

38 "Ever Dream This Man?" http://www.thisman.org/history/.

39 Heidi Hollis. *The Hat Man: The True Story of Evil Encounters.* (Peabody, MA: Level Head Publishing, 2014).

Man. He incites fear, a sense of dread, and even hopelessness. Hollis notes that dreams of the Hat Man are recorded worldwide. He mostly observes, then fades or walks away.

In late December 2016, we received an e-mail from a woman who said she'd experienced forty years of strange experiences with other worldly beings who often haunted her dreams. Jules wrote to explain a synchronicity related to the Hat Man phenomenon. "One day years back, I was talking with some friends and one of the women said she had a weird experience, waking to find someone in her room one night. The description she gave was of a tall male wearing what seemed to be a top hat and cape. He didn't do anything or say anything—he was just there."

Jules had nearly forgotten about the story until one night when she experienced something similar that began with what she described as a common sleep paralysis dream event. Not only was she unable to move, but her body was vibrating. "I was consciously fighting to move, and the more I fought the stronger the vibration and the paralysis became. I finally managed to shift to a slightly bent L-position on the bed and fought to open my eyes."

What she saw shocked her. "There was a light coming in through the window, and the shadow of a tall man wearing what seemed to be a cape and some kind of hat, standing at the foot of the bed nearer to the wall. Nothing was said, nothing happened, but I shouted at him in my head to get out of my room, at which time there was a frightful screech like a big bird. At that point, I woke up and could move my body."

As Jules thought about it, she remembered the woman's story about a similar unwanted visitor. She wondered if her unconscious mind had dredged up the memory and played it out in a dream. Some years later, she would reject that scenario after hearing about another Hat Man dream.

"I was subbing at a school in North Carolina when a girl in one of my classes started talking about her odd phobias. She feared this, she feared that, and oddly enough she had a fear of Abe Lincoln.

"I asked her later why Abe Lincoln and she told me about a very strange event in her life. She woke up one night, and there at the foot of the bed was a tall man with a cape and a hat, and he reminded her of Lincoln. He didn't say anything, he didn't do anything. He was just there."

That made three Hat Man dreams, her own and two others that were told directly to her rather than through a third party. Jules found that uncanny, and a meaningful coincidence. While her experience is clearly unusual, an Internet search reveals that the Hat Man has made appearances to dreamers throughout the world. Like Jules's student, most of the people writing about this dark entity were terrified. Some even say they felt this malevolent being feeding on their terror. Others saw not only a shadowy figure, but red glowing eyes.

The Hat Man phenomenon opens numerous questions about spirit contact. The shadowy figure appears in dreams and seemingly emerges briefly into conscious awareness. Does the Hat Man exist as an independent entity? Is there more than one such entity? What does he or they want? While it's difficult to pinpoint the intent of such a being, we can look at the best possible outcome of an encounter. Once beyond the fear, we can understand that our encounter with the dark side allows us to better recognize and appreciate the light.

PRACTICE 22: TRACKING YOUR DREAMING SPIRIT

If we think of ourselves as spirits on a human journey rather than humans on a spiritual journey, it's easy to recognize our dreaming self as part of the spirit world. If you've been tracking your dreams in your journal, look them over to see if you can find any dreams in which you describe your appearance as well as your actions and feelings. If you can't find any clear descriptions, you can incubate your dream so that you will become aware of your dreaming self.

Keep in mind that your answers will vary from dream to dream. But a pattern related to your behavior in waking life may emerge if you track several dreams. Here are some questions to ask yourself, and include in your journal, once you've focused on your dreaming self.

- What do you look like? Are you the same person as in your waking life? If not, how are you different in appearance?

- Are you present and involved in the dream actions or just observing?

- Do you direct the action or are you carried along by events?

- Are you acting the same as you do during your waking life or do you do things you would never try in waking life?

9

❋

Spirit of
the Shamans

SHAMANISM HAS BEEN called the world's oldest religion, dating back tens of thousands of years. It's not a religion in the traditional sense, because there is no faith or belief required. Rather, it's the oldest healing system, and was part of all indigenous cultures. It's about direct contact with spiritual realms, not only by the shaman, but also those seeking help and healing. The client or patient is an active participant, pursuing visions, possibly encountering other realities.

Shamanism lives on among surviving indigenous cultures and has been adapted in the West, often blending ancient practices with modern psychology. While ritual practices vary among shamanic schools, healing and spirit communication through rituals and journeys remain at the heart of Western shamanism.

Mind Stuff

Western shamans, like their traditional counterparts, seek altered states of consciousness for healing and spirit contact. The altered states are typically achieved through chanting, meditations, fire rituals, and other practices. Vision quests, which are usually associated with initiation into shamanism, involve extended periods of isolation in nature and are aimed at achieving an important personal vision through an altered state.

Throughout history, hallucinogenic drugs have played a role in shamanism in many traditional cultures. Generally speaking, Western shamans avoid promoting drug use, but some partake in such rituals, usually when joining with traditional shamans in their home territory, particularly in the Amazon basin where ayahuasca is the drug of choice.

Medicine Wheel

At the heart of Western shamanism are medicine wheel rituals, a healing practice that invokes archetypal spirit powers related to the four cardinal directions. From an archaeological perspective, medicine wheels were circles made with rocks by Native American people. Usually, there was a center point with spires of rock extending out and dividing the circle into at least four parts. The Bighorn Medicine Wheel, thought to be the largest known, spans eighty feet in diameter and is between three hundred to eight hundred years old. From above, it looks like a bicycle wheel with spokes.

While the original purpose of these wheels remains a mystery, it's thought that medicine wheels served as physical manifestation of spiritual energy, and were used by shamans in healing ceremonies. Indeed, indigenous traditions have carried on medicine wheel healings, with varying interpretations of the cardinal points.

Alberto Villoldo, a medical anthropologist and author, adapted the shamanic traditions he learned in Peru from Qّero Indians, who are descendants of the Incas. In the late 1980s, Villoldo began to translate medicine wheel teachings into a Western framework, which he refers to as "a psychology of the sacred,"[40] and later founded the Four Winds Society.

---

40   Alberto Villoldo and Erik Jendresen. *Island of the Sun: Mastering the Inca Medicine Wheel.* (Rochester, VT: Destiny Books, 1992), 25.

He realized that "the Four Winds represented an ancient formula for transformation: shed the past that restrains us, confront and overcome the fears of the future and death that paralyze us, and we may live fully in the present; apply the skills learned along the way to access a sea of consciousness as vast as time itself, then find a vehicle for expressing the experience with beauty and living as a caretaker of the Earth."[41]

Here is a brief trip around the medicine wheel in the Q'ero version, which features archetypal images related to the cardinal points. [42]

- The journey begins in the south in the home of the Serpent, where you heal old wounds and traumas by shedding the past like the Serpent sheds its skin.

- Moving to the west, you encounter the Jaguar, who teaches you about life, death, and rebirth. You embrace what's coming your way. It's about moving beyond fear, anger, guilt, and shame. It's about facing fear and overcoming it. You release old, outmoded ways.

- In the north, you meet the Hummingbird and engage ancient wisdom and knowledge. You learn to manifest the impossible and to receive help from ancestors. You reconnect with nature.

- In the east, you encounter the archetype of the Condor as you summon your destiny. It's about the big picture, and the way of the visionary. The Condor guides you into the role and responsibility of cocreator.

In the Western world, medicine wheels are a way to balance emotional, mental, physical, and spiritual aspects of our lives. Rituals and meditation

---

41   Ibid., 25.

42   Jon Rassmussen. "Medicine Wheel: The Primary Cultures Healing Journey." http://www.dreamingintobeing.com/about-shamanism/the-medicine-wheel/.

are the mechanisms for pursuing the heart of the medicine wheel and unraveling its mysteries. But you don't need to follow any particular formula. You can create your own personalized medicine wheel.

PRACTICE 23: FINDING YOUR PERSONAL MEDICINE WHEEL

Find a private open area where you can create a circle at least six feet in diameter. You can create it with stones or other common objects, such as fruit. For one of Rob's meditation workshops at a yoga studio, he created a medicine circle made up of mangos from the trees in your backyard. Divide the circle into four segments by creating a cross using the same objects. Align the cross with the four cardinal directions. You will face the cardinal direction of your choice. Each of the directions should be a separate meditation.

Shamanic meditations are typically accompanied by repetitive drumming, rattles, or other percussion instruments that move you into a meditative/trance state. You can download shamanic drumming by searching that term or *shamanic journeys* on the Internet. It's best to listen to the rhythmic percussion through headphones or earbuds.

As the shamanic beat resonates through your body, think about the direction you will meditate on. Maybe you light a candle in honor of the cardinal direction. When you're ready, imagine a large circular opening in a grove of trees. Inside the circle is a medicine wheel made of white stones with two lines of stones inside the circle that are aligned with the cardinal points.

Picture yourself at the center of the medicine wheel and see yourself surrounded by ancestors or benevolent light beings. You can remain seated or after a couple of minutes you can settle onto your back. If you lie down, the direction should be at your feet. If you sit up, you would face it.

Take several long, slow, deep breaths as you relax your entire body. When you're fully relaxed, you can move on. As you move from relaxation into your journey, pose these questions:

- What is the significance of this direction for me?
- How will this energy help me on my path?
- Is there a spirit guide for this path?
- What are the stories for this direction?

When the drumming slows, draw back from your journey, expressing gratitude for all the knowledge and guidance you received. In your journal, create a section called *Medicine Wheel*, and write what you remember from your experience. Note how it relates to the direction. If your results were minimal, you might want to go back to the same direction on your next meditation. Alternately, you might try a new direction and return to this one later. As you write in your journal, add any stories of your own about the direction. For example, if you traveled north on a trip, what experiences come to mind?

You can explore any of the four winds, as the Q'eros refer to the cardinal points, at any time. It's an ongoing journey.

In 1994, Rob went on a vision quest with Villoldo and others from the Four Winds Society. Near the end of the four-day journey, he perched atop a large boulder and gazed over a branch of Canyon de Chelly on the Navajo Nation. He didn't move for half an hour. In his vision, he soared over the canyon, aware of the presence of spirits. He was ecstatic, free of his body, launched on a shamanic journey, accompanied by spirit guides. Where would he go? What would he experience?

A distant voice cried out to him. He tried to ignore it, but the voice turned more urgent. It pulled him back to the boulder. He heard it again as his awareness returned fully to his body and he glanced over his shoulder. It was time to leave and the others waited in the van at the rim. They'd been calling to him from the rim of the canyon, trying to pull him out of his trance. He and the others had undergone long days of hiking through the canyon, setting up camp, followed by shamanic rituals that carried on late into the night. The combination resulted in an array of mystical experiences that had lasting effects on his life.

He would go on to write four novels with Native American and shamanic themes, one of which won the Edgar Allan Poe Award, sponsored by the Mystery Writers of America, and another that was a finalist for the award. Meditation became a regular part of his life, and as a meditation instructor at a yoga studio, he occasionally teaches workshops in shamanic meditations and lucid dreaming.

Typically, in Native American cultures, teenage boys were sent on vision quests in which they would spend up to four days isolated in nature, oftentimes without supplies. Their quest was to seek spiritual guidance and direction for their lives. During a vision or Big Dream—the term for a life-changing dream experience—they might encounter a guardian animal, a spirit guide, or a force of nature.

The Big Dream

From the shaman's perspective, there are ordinary dreams and Big Dreams. The shaman is interested in the latter. Big Dreams involve communication with a guardian spirit or power animal. "A Big Dream is one that is repeated several times in the same basic way on different nights or it is a one-time dream that is so vivid that it is like being awake," writes anthropologist Michael Harner in his classic book *The Way of the Shaman.* [43]

Since the publication of his book in 1990, Harner has taught shamanic techniques to thousands of students at workshops. He describes a shaman as "a man or woman who enters an altered state of consciousness—at will—to contact and utilize an ordinarily hidden reality in order to acquire knowledge, power, and to help other persons." [44]

---

43   Michael Harner. *The Way of the Shaman.* (New York: Harper One), 1990, 99.
44   Ibid., 20.

The difference between a shamanic dream or Big Dream and a lucid dream is that the former deals with spirit or guardian contact with the intent of gaining power or knowledge. A lucid dream is typically an adventure or journey that is not necessarily connected with any spiritual tradition or related goal.

In his book, Harner relates a Big Dream recounted by a woman who took one of his workshops. In the dream, she was in a car accident in which she hit metal twice but wasn't seriously injured. About a month later, she was driving with her son when a car veered in front of her. She struck the car, was spun around, and struck it again. As the car spun, she was aware of being pinned against her son, but also being outside and just above the car watching her dream unfold. As the accident unfolded, she felt a sense of deep peace, of being protected by a guardian spirit, who was present and protecting her from danger.

The Journeys

In shamanism, meditations are referred to as *journeys* and the journeys can take you into other worlds, known as the Lower, Middle, and Upper Worlds. Such journeys provide a bridge between our everyday world and the spirit world.

Of course, these worlds don't exist in the same sense as our physical world. Shamans interpret them as places, even though the spirit world is nowhere...and everywhere. But how real is our physical world? Its existence is based on our perception, our sight, hearing, touch, and other senses. We have a sense of physical reality, but there are endless interpretations of what we sense. Politics provides a great example of extreme differences in interpretations of what is real. Eastern traditions tell us that our physical reality is a collective illusion or dream.

The spirit worlds of shamanism are a source of healing, power, and information for those who explore these realms. The guides we encounter are protective spirits, there to assist us. They are not interested in directing, dominating, or controlling us.

Traditional cultures designated these spirit worlds in the distant past, long before recorded history, long before Christianity. The Lower World is *not* hell and the Upper World is *not* heaven. The Lower World is a place where you can meet the archetypal or universal, mythical beings—the jester, the magician, the sage—and other spirits known through mythology. In a sense, the Lower World is a spiritual source for all of nature. On a journey to this realm, you might encounter pre-historic beasts, like the saber-toothed tiger or the mammoth, that no longer exist. Or you might find a field of unicorns and winged horses.

Once you have a grasp of the nature of shamanism, you can enroll in a shamanic workshop to learn more and take part in group journeys. Of course, you also can explore these other worlds on your own.

For any shamanic journey, it's a good idea to call on spirit guides or power animals—known and unknown—to place a veil of protection around you. These beings, when asked, can offer very powerful protection. Also, express gratitude and respect in advance for their help.

Here are guided meditations to the three worlds of shamanism that Rob has used in his meditation workshop series that explores a variety of types and styles of meditation.

PRACTICE 24: THE LOWER WORLD MEDITATION

Settle into a place where you feel comfortable and won't be interrupted. Turn on your shamanic drumming, wearing your headphones or ear-buds. Take your time moving into a relaxed state. Don't forget to take several deep breaths. Follow the drumming and allow it to take you into a trance-like state.

When you're ready, imagine a place in nature that appeals to you. It could be mountains or forest. Notice your surroundings. Find your way to a nearby stream and follow it. Keep walking until you realize you're standing near the top of a waterfall that flows down into a pool. You can see the spray in the air forming a rainbow.

You notice flagstone steps going down along the edge of the water-fall and follow them. Now you see a path that goes behind the waterfall. You step inside the curtain of water and into a cavern. You see a tunnel ahead and light coming from deep within the cavern. You walk toward it as the floor descends deeper and deeper into the earth.

You reach an opening and when you come out on the other side, you find yourself in another world, a place in nature with dramatic scenery, mountains and forest, lakes and rocks. It's as if you've entered a primordial version of earth. It feels different from the world you left. The landscape is vibrant and filled with life. Your senses take in the richness of this world, and you start to see the beings that inhabit the Lower World.

There's a large tree nearby with an enormous canopy and next to it is your guide. It could be a power animal or person, or a mythical character from ancient times. Approach the guide and greet the being. Pay attention to what happens on your journey, how you feel, any sensations you experience. You might receive a verbal message, but it might also come through events and scenery. Notice if it's day or night, or if the sun is out or hidden. What's the weather like? Notice how your guardian acts, and any smells, tastes, sounds. It's all part of the message. Express your gratitude to the guide.

When the drumming slows down, it brings you back into your everyday world. You might write about your experience in a journal. It will help you remember and assist you in future journeys.

Practice 25: The Upper World Meditation

Rob once talked to a young man who had been bitten by a coral snake and fell into a coma for a couple of days. When he recovered, he described a fantastic out-of-body experience that felt more real than this life. He visited a majestic crystal city—an impossible city without foundations. He called it the most awesome place that anyone could ever visit, and he wanted to tell everyone he met about it. The people looked human, but they were more than human.

His experience sounded very similar to a journey to the Upper World. Fortunately, you don't have to get bitten by a poisonous snake to travel there.

You can access the Upper World in shamanic meditation through a similar process as you followed with the Lower World. Once you relax and turn on your drumming accompaniment, imagine yourself in a pristine environment in nature. Maybe it's a mountainous forest or a tranquil beach at the edge of the ocean. See it, smell the air, feel a gentle breeze, notice the lighting. Is it morning, noon, or evening?

This time, instead of burrowing into the earth, you're going to rise into the sky by climbing a rope or ladder, floating off in a hot air balloon, soaring away on the wings of a large bird, or leaping from a high cliff.

You continue rising and rising, higher and higher, until you come to a region of fog. You pass through it, and on the other side you enter the Upper World. You might find yourself in a crystal city or a city of clouds. Spirits in human form reside in this higher realm and serve as teachers for explorers who make the journey. They answer questions and help us develop spiritual knowledge and wisdom.

Here you'll meet a guide who will answer any questions. Remember, the advice you receive is something you can accept or reject. Consider it closely, but make sure it feels right before you act on what you've been told.

When the drumming slows, you can return to your place of meditation by the same means as you ascended. In your journal, note the date and describe your feelings and what you discovered on your journey.

PRACTICE 26: THE MIDDLE WORLD MEDITATION

The Middle World is a hidden aspect of our world. It's a realm where the spirits of all living things exist and where these spirits develop the ability to shift into physical form. It's also a place where thoughts easily manifest into reality. It's here where our unconscious minds create our collective reality, which includes plenty of undesirable conditions that come into our personal experience.

While the Middle World offers us the opportunity to create harmony in our lives and attract what we want, it's also a place where spirits of the dead cling to Earth, and where negative energy resides. In spite of these hazards, you can visit this realm safely to improve your life. But it's important to focus on all things that are positive, and not on anything that would cause harm.

The Middle World is also the home of ancient nature spirits, including fairies, elves, dwarves, gnomes, mermaids and mermen, plant devas, elemental nature spirits, and the beings of fairy tales, dreams, and fantasies. These beings, which are considered mythical in our daily world, can assist you in bringing balance and harmony into your life.

An opportune time to explore the Middle World in meditation is when you are searching for a lost item or looking for information that can't be easily found in the everyday world of Google. The process of entering the Middle World is similar to the one you followed for finding your way into the Lower World. However, to avoid confusion it's a good idea to use a different means of entering the earth. For example, if you entered the Lower World through a tunnel after opening a trapdoor hidden in the ground, you might reach the Middle World by descending through the hollow trunk of an ancient tree or diving into a deep pool of water.

You pass through the tunnel into the Middle World where again you'll be met by a guide or guides. The guide will show you what it is you seek, and then you return the same way you entered. While the experience is still fresh in your mind, write down what you learned and how you felt about what happened.

A Shaman's Predictions

What's it like working with a shaman? That depends on the shaman and your circumstances, but one thing is for sure: it won't be like anything you've experienced with a psychic or healer.

When Arizona sculptor and artist Lauren Raines was going through a divorce, she heard about an energy healer and herbalist in Crownsville, Maryland, who had studied with renowned Western shaman Sandra Ingerman. She was at a point in her life where she was "very open to anything," and went to him for a soul retrieval.

The shamanic practice of soul retrieval helps to regain a soul that has become trapped, disconnected, or lost through some sort of trauma. Depending on the circumstances, a divorce can certainly qualify as a trauma.

"He was very businesslike, and without knowing anything about me, put on his drums tape and headset, had me lie down next to him, and we tranced together. At the end of the session he *blew soul fragments* back into my body, and we talked about what he saw. We talked about cutting the cords from my ex-husband, and my former community that I'd left when I moved. He concluded the session by telling me: 'You'll know it's all over when you see a magenta flower that looks like a cosmos, and a terra cotta angel.'"

Eight months later, Lauren crossed the country with all her possessions and her cat loaded into her van. She was determined to move back to Berkeley, California, and start a new life. She had decided she would sleep in her van if necessary until she found somewhere to move.

"I began my adventure as soon as I arrived with a visit to a coffee house I last visited twenty years earlier. Almost immediately I was greeted by a long-ago friend, who recognized me, bought me a cup of coffee, and offered me a place to stay. I didn't have to spend a single night in my van, and when I walked into his living room there was a huge photograph of a magenta cosmos flower hanging above his fireplace!"

A few months later, Lauren answered an ad for a roommate. "I walked into a house with an altar, and in the center of it was a terra cotta angel." She knew she'd found the right place, especially after she discovered that her new roommate was a colleague of Starhawk, a woman she admired. "Starhawk's writings were the foundation of my MFA thesis more than a decade earlier. Just like that, my new life began, and I ended up working with the very people I most wanted to work with, never having had to even try! The shaman was entirely right in his prediction."

The shaman gave Lauren two specific bits of information about markers that would signal when her transitional period was finished— the magenta cosmos flower and the terra cotta angel. How was he able to see something so precise for a woman he had just met?

"Shamans are inspired visionaries who are able to access information through their invisible allies for the benefit of themselves, their families, and their communities. This process is known as divination, and it is usually accomplished through ceremony and ritual," wrote Sandra Ingerman and Hank Wesselman in *Awakening to the Spirit World*.[45] "Through their relationship with these transpersonal forces, shamans are able to retrieve lost power and restore it to its original owners."

Through the trance-state the shaman and Lauren entered together, he was able to retrieve the power Lauren had lost and was allowed to see the most probable path her future would take.

PRACTICE 27: POWER ANIMAL MEDITATION

Shamans consider animal spirits to be powerful allies in their healing work and call on them frequently. They might beckon a variety of animals if the circumstances call for it, but usually they consider one particular type of animal their power animal. If you are drawn to a particular species—a dolphin, a jaguar, an eagle, whatever—then you

---

45   Sandra Ingerman and Hank Wesselman. *Awakening to the Spirit World: The Shamanic Path of Direct Revelation*. (Boulder, CO: Sounds True, 2010), 89–90.

might've already found your power animal. If not, try this meditation for uncovering your power animal.

When a power animal appears in a vision, you are encountering the archetype, soul, or essence of that animal, not an individual animal. The meaning associated with that animal should resonate with you. Think of the animal as a powerful ally, a guiding force.

Settle into your place for meditation, either sitting or lying on your back. Turn on your shamanic beat, as previously described. You might cover your eyes with a bandana or other eye cover.

Take a few deep breaths, relaxing your body from head to toe. When you're ready, imagine you're walking down a trail through a pristine setting in nature. Take a few moments to locate it. Maybe it's a place you've visited before.

Let the drumming move you into a deeper meditative state. Pay attention to each step you take. Is the ground soft and spongy or dry and rocky? Is the path gentle or rugged? After a time, you come to a large rock with an oval indentation. It looks like the perfect place to sit and rest.

Notice your surroundings. What time of day is it? Is the sun shining? Is it overcast? Warm or cool? Be aware of details. As you rest on your boulder, watch for any sign of animal life in your surroundings, either on the ground or in the trees. An animal might appear that seems curious about you. Greet the creature. Think of it as a new friend, your power animal. Rather than an individual animal, you are actually encountering the spirit or archetype of this creature that can serve as your guide and protector.

Stay in this place and enjoy your surroundings until the drumming slows, calling you back. Give thanks to any beings that appeared, any messages that were received. Retrace your steps along the path, and fully return to your ordinary awareness.

Animal Wisdom

If you've found your power animal, it's time to explore the meaning of the creature you encountered. Here's a brief guide to some prominent power animals and the wisdom they project. You can search for other animals in various totem guides, many of which are available on the Internet. Besides understanding the essence of your own power animal, you can use such guides to find the meaning of animals you might encounter during your daily life.

Bear

Bear medicine is about conserving energy, deep rest, and rejuvenation. It's exploration of a solitary nature. Bear suggests you back off somewhat and let life come to you. Slow down, reorganize your plans, and retire to your cave to meditate. Alternately, bear is telling you to stop hiding and get out into the world. You're well equipped to tackle the challenges.

Attributes:

- Power and strength

- Solitude

- Rejuvenation

- Seeker of visions

- Individuality

- Recovery

Crow

Crow medicine is a gateway between light and dark, fear and hope. The crow reminds you that you have the freedom to choose. You sculpt your world as you see fit, confronting fear and overcoming it, or fleeing it only to face it again. Positive thinking allows you to solve problems in creative ways. Clarity in your thoughts leads to self-empowerment and understanding.

Attributes:

- Working without fear in darkness
- Moving through space and time
- Carrier of souls from darkness into light
- Moving freely through the void
- Guidance while working in shadow
- Honoring ancestors
- Understanding all things related to ethics

Dolphin

Dolphin medicine encourages you to live in the moment and relish it for all it's worth. It's time to add joy and playfulness into whatever you do. It may signal the beginning of a sexual relationship that, above all else, is fun and playful. Dolphin medicine is ideal for delving more deeply into your creativity. Allow the intuitive and spiritual dimensions of your life to shine through. Use your intuitive knowing to find your purpose and pursue it. But have fun with it!

Attributes:

- Balance and harmony
- Wisdom
- Knowledge of the sea
- Freedom
- Communication skills
- Trust

Dragonfly

Is she a dragon or a fly? She's a master of illusion and seems to shimmer in her iridescent body armor, echoing the shifting nature of reality. Dragonfly in her very essence suggests our world is a realm of dreams and illusion. Through dragonfly, you can see the truth in a matter. Dragonfly is a master of flight, hovering, moving forward and back. She represents swiftness, change and elusiveness, and often acts as a messenger. It also represents transformation, a more sexually active time in your life, and that you're in the process of shedding your old worldview. Your spiritual beliefs are moving toward something new that will enable you to fulfill your enormous potential.

Attributes:

- Understanding dreams

- Breaking down illusions

- Seeing the truth

- Swiftness and change

- Power of flight

Eagle

Eagle medicine tells you it's time to reconnect with your spiritual path. You can rise above any problem. You're able to place things in their proper perspective. Self-examination and looking within is in order. Eagle also teaches you to stay grounded, even when you are flying high. Your intuition and clairvoyance are heightened.

Attributes:

- Strength and courage

- Opportunities

- Wisdom

- Healing
- Visualizing spiritual realms
- Connecting to spirit guides
- Power and balance
- Seeing the big picture

Elephant

Elephant medicine is about dealing with your emotions. You feel things deeply. Family is important, especially the little ones and the older ones. You desire to serve others, but need to nurture yourself as well. You remain loyal to others despite any difficulties that arise. This medicine portends increased good health and the loyalty of friends and family, of your "herd."

Attributes:
- Strength and intelligence
- Connecting with ancient wisdom
- Confidence
- Removing obstacles
- Patience
- Royalty

Frog

Frog medicine recognizes the power of transformation. This spirit animal supports us in times of change. Frog is strongly associated with water and connects us with emotions and feminine energies. Frog medicine is about cleansing, physical or emotional healing, and also sensitivity toward one's environment. It often appears when a transformative event is on its way into our lives.

Attributes:

- Cleansing

- Renewal, rebirth

- Fertility, abundance

- Transformation, metamorphosis

- Life mysteries and ancient wisdom

Hawk

Hawk is a messenger from the spirit world. Hawk medicine allows you to see matters from a higher perspective, using the power of observation. You gain illumination, which allows you to solve your problems and to develop spiritual awareness. With this medicine, your grace and agility are heightened.

Attributes:

- Farsighted

- Illumination

- Messenger from spirit

- Recalling past lives

- Creativity

- Truth-seeker

- Courage

- Overcoming problems

Horse

Horse medicine enhances your inner strength and can become a driving force in your life. It's about personal power, passion, and the desire for freedom. The energy is long-lasting, powerful. It's also about the ability to overcome obstacles and pursue your goals.

Attributes:

- Strong emotions

- Passionate desires

- Physical strength

- Vitality

- Ability to succeed

Hummingbird

Hummingbird medicine invites you to savor the sweetness of life. It lifts you from negativity and usually augurs well for joy, improved health, and the fruition of dreams. It helps you to express love more fully in your daily life. Swift and adaptable with its high velocity wing movements, the hummingbird can fly long distances, and can even fly backwards. Hummingbird teaches you to keep a playful and optimistic outlook and to find joy in everything you do. When hummingbirds act as spirit messengers, they communicate joy and happiness from your loved ones who have passed.

Attributes:
- Adaptable

- Resilient

- Optimistic

- Lightness of being

- Bringing joy into life

- Ability to respond quickly

Jaguar, Mountain Lion, Cougar, Florida Panther

The message of the big cats is about power. You have the ability to work independently or as part of a group, especially if you're in a leadership position. The big cat medicine allows you to embark on your own quest. You hold your own when confronted by others who disagree with you. These cats signal you're on the right path and that it's to your benefit to remain elusive.

Attributes:

- Gaining self-confidence
- Cunning
- Using power wisely and without ego
- Balancing power, intention, strength
- Freedom from guilt
- Empowering oneself
- Moving ahead in the dark without fear
- Seeing patterns within chaos
- Exploring unknown places
- Shape-shifting
- "Seeing" distant events

Lion

A relentless fighter, the lion spirit represents courage and strength. Lion medicine is about overcoming difficulties. Lions also symbolize challenging emotions, such as anger or fear. Lion medicine usually signals your family is important to you. Family may be your blood family or a larger community of like-minded individuals, your "tribe."

Attributes:

- Courage

- Strength

- Group activities

- Personal power

- Animal magnetism

Owl

The message of the owl is about overcoming fears, maneuvering through the darkness, seeing what is hidden, and paying attention to cues in your environment. Owl medicine offers wisdom and skills you need. You can access information that's hidden from others. Be alert for news coming your way. Owl is also a messenger between the living and the dead.

Attributes:

- Intuition

- Wisdom

- Exploring the unknown

- Inspiration and guidance

- Cutting through illusion

- Seeing through deceit

Snake

Snake medicine relates to an exploration of the mysteries of life. It deals with psychic energy and creative powers, shedding the past and releasing old patterns of behavior and thought. Seeing a snake in a vision could also be a cue that you are ready for a deep shamanic journey, a journey of healing and renewal. Your spiritual activities are heightened with snake medicine, your dreams become more lucid, and your sexuality is deepened. Snake is a spirit of transformation, of life and death.

Attributes:

- Healing energy

- Creative power

- Guidance on shamanic journeys

- Shedding old ways

- Letting go of the past

- Dealing with pain

- Exploring the unknown

- Life force, primal energy

Turtle and Tortoise

Turtle medicine suggests slowing down, taking a break from your busy life, and getting grounded. Just as the turtle travels with its home, you want to feel comfortable wherever you go. Rather than bursts of energy in your spiritual search, the turtle suggests a grounded series of steps moving toward transformation. Tortoise is an ancient seeker of wisdom and a treasure hunter. It symbolizes longevity, perseverance, and immortality.

Attributes:

- Self-reliance

- Tenacity

- Patience

- Persistence

- Psychic protection

- Expert navigation
- Ancient knowledge

Whale

Whale medicine is all about communication, often with distant sources. It allows you to hear what's actually being said. If you're dealing with something too big to handle on your own, whale medicine advises you to get some help. Don't allow pride to keep you from asking others for help or advice or from sharing your worries with someone else. This totem is about going deep within yourself to awaken your inner creativity. When the whale sleeps, one hemisphere of its brain remains awake, then it switches sides. The message is that you should pay attention to both the logical and intuitive sides of your brain.

Attributes:
- Creative
- Power
- Magic
- Nurturing
- Appreciation for beauty
- Emotional depth and clarity
- Well-being

Wolf

Wolves generally are group-oriented and hunt together in a pack. But a sense of independence is also part of wolf medicine. It's about establishing yourself in the community or group setting, working cooperatively, being both teacher and student. Wolf is about giving others space to make their own decisions Be open to new knowledge and skills and leave space for others to make their own decisions (i.e., don't control other people).

Attributes:

- Teacher/guide

- Fearless confidence

- Working together while maintaining independence

- Communication

- Working in harmony

- Sharing knowledge in a structured way

Power of the Orishas

With the rise of Christianity over the past two millennia, efforts were made to wipe out Pagan practices. Some shamanic practitioners went underground. In the case of the Q'ero Indians of the Andes, that meant the tribe resettled at nearly fourteen thousand feet above sea level. As a result, the Q'eros avoided conquistadors and missionaries, and retained their spirits and culture.

Other forms of shamanism actually hid within Christianity and eventually merged with it. That was the case of Yoruba people enslaved in West Africa and transported to the New World. The syncretism of ancient African gods with Catholic saints resulted in Santeria—which means worship of the saints. The practice is best known in Cuba and, more recently, in Hispanic communities in Florida and elsewhere in the US.

The saints are known as *orishas,* archetypal beings with specific qualities that can be called upon. Saint Barbara, for instance, became the god Changó, the great warrior who governs fire and lightning. Saint Anthony became Elegguá, the second most powerful of the seven primary gods, who opens and closes doors of opportunity.

Like other shamanic practitioners, santeros—the priests or practitioners of Santeria—interact with the orishas and the spirit world to gain insight, to heal, and to predict the future. Everything is believed to be the result of spiritual forces—both good and evil. Even though Santeria is not widely known in the US outside of Florida, ironically during the 1950s and 1960s, one of the orishas, Babalú-Ayé, patron of the sick, was frequently invoked in song on the popular television series *I Love Lucy* by Cuban actor Desi Arnaz.

Besides working with the orishas, santeros also mingle with *seres* or spirit guides when they go into trance. The seres take over the body of the santeros and are capable of performing healings and physical actions that often defy known laws of nature.

Encounter with a Santero

The santero, wearing white cotton pants and shirt, motioned us to follow him into a back room. We'd been waiting nearly an hour in a modest house in Miami's Little Havana.

We entered a room with several chairs and an altar that featured carved statuettes of a black Madonna and a Native American shaman, candles, stones, amulets, vases of flowers, a bowl of candy, and another of fruit smothered in honey. Something primitive and ancient permeated the air. The carcass of a dead chicken lay in one corner, a sacrifice apparently performed for another client. We noticed there wasn't a single drop of blood on the floor.

Ruben Delgado took off his shoes and rolled up his loose cotton pants to just below his knees as he prepared to make way for Francisco, his *ser* or spirit guide, who would take possession of his body. This was the way Francisco had dressed, Delgado explained. He described Francisco as a very old black man with a bad left leg. He was brought to Cuba from the Congo as a slave in the early 1800s and died in 1870.

We were curious outsiders with no past experience with Santeria, but interested in meeting Francisco. Delgado was a handsome man of twenty-seven with Latino features and coal-black hair. The year was 1984, and he had arrived from Cuba three years earlier and spoke very little English. Trish, who grew up in Venezuela, translated. We had no idea what was about to occur and what followed was so powerful and shocking it made us believers in this type of shamanism.

When a santero's spirit guides go to work on the malign forces that are causing a client's problems, it's as if your body and soul become a spiritual battleground. The spirits deal with health problems, love and romance issues, career and financial challenges, karma, and even spirit attachment and possession.

Several personalities manifested when Delgado was in trance. Francisco, who died more than two hundred years ago, typically opened the gate for others to "ride the horse," as he referred to Delgado. The transformation he underwent could be clinically diagnosed as multiple personality disorder.

In fact, that was what happened to Delgado when he was a child. At age twelve, he experienced violent convulsions that were diagnosed as epileptic seizures. While he was hospitalized, a woman told his mother that conventional methods would never cure him because the convulsions were caused by a spirit guide attempting to possess him. But Delgado's family continued the medical treatment and his condition worsened. One night, following a particularly violent seizure, he spontaneously entered a trance and Francisco spoke for the first time.

During our observations of Delgado in a trance, we witnessed his transformation to Francisco as he bent down and snapped his fingers near the floor. We later learned that in his life, Francisco had a pet snake and that was how he called the snake. What was most startling, though, was Francisco's apparent ability to defy physical laws, as we know them, while he was *riding* Delgado.

Physically, Delgado's body changed, his spine became bent and crooked, his facial expressions were like those of an old man, his voice deepened, the way he spoke slowed. On two occasions he ground the glowing end of a cigar along his forearm and when the ashes were washed away, there were no visible burn marks. He claimed he felt no pain. We also witnessed Delgado, as Francisco, gulp down about a third of a bottle of rum, smash the empty bottle on the tile floor, then dance barefoot on the broken glass. He exhibited no sign of pain or bleeding. Delgado later told us that he didn't drink alcohol because he had no tolerance for it. Except when Francisco was around!

But whether Delgado's trance personalities were external entities— as they appeared to be to us—a part of himself, or even deft fakery, his clients were convinced he created positive changes in their lives.

Take the case of Jorge, who traveled from Tampa to visit Delgado.

A Healing Session

When Jorge requested Delgado's assistance, he was suffering from depression, spells of memory loss, and high blood pressure. When he arrived at Delgado's house in Little Havana, Delgado was dressed completely in white, a color that he said is ideal for his work because of its purity and clarity. He rolled his loose cotton pants to just below the knees and removed his shoes. Francisco, he explained, preferred working barefoot.

He lit several candles and sprinkled the room and everyone in it with Florida Water, a light cologne used for spiritual cleansing. He puffed on a thick maduro cigar and blew clouds of smoke around his chair. Santeros believe that cigar smoke, like certain types of cologne, releases beneficial energy.

Seated on a chair in the center of the room with a blue cloth spread across his lap, Delgado recited the Lord's Prayer and then chanted a spiritual mass that begins with prayers compiled by Allan Kardec, a nineteenth-century French philosopher and Spiritualist.

As Delgado chanted, his voice gradually increased in pitch and his breathing quickened. Fifteen minutes after starting the ritual, his body convulsed as if jolted by electrical shocks. Spittle ran from the corners of his mouth; the cigar fell to the floor, and his shoulders slumped. When he spoke again, his words were slurred and guttural and he used phrases that were not part of Delgado's ordinary speech. Men, for instance, were called *pantalones* (pants) and women were called *faldas* (skirts). Francisco had arrived.

Without raising his head or opening his eyes, he told Jorge that he had attracted a negative influence that inhabited the house. To exorcise the evil spirit, he began with a cleansing, passing white flowers along the sides of his body, over his head, and across the soles of his feet. Soon the floor was strewn with petals.

The chanting continued as Francisco linked arms with Jorge so they were back to back. Rocking forward, he lifted him off the floor and they twirled around three times as he demanded the evil spirit leave. The house was then blessed and cleansed in the name of the orishas.

Over the subsequent weeks and months, Jorge's health issues started clearing up. His memory improved, his depression lifted, he changed his diet and started walking briskly each day. His blood pressure normalized.

If Jorge hadn't been a believer in the power of a santero's spirit guide to heal, would Delgado's rituals have had any effect on his health? Is belief a critical element in this type of healing? That depends.

An avowed skeptic—someone who doesn't believe in the afterlife or spirits, who believes we have one life and when we're dead, that's all—probably wouldn't be swayed by a spirit healing session. But a person on the fence about the reality of Spirit and spirit contact might be more open to it, particularly if the person had been diagnosed with a health issue or a disease. When your health or the health of a loved one is at risk, it's likelier you'll be open to anything—even a healing from Spirit.

Preparing for a Mediumistic Reading

Maybe you've never had a reading with a medium, but would like to try one. It doesn't have to be someone as exotic as a santero or shaman.

There are many people with mediumistic abilities who offer readings. Some are very good, others so-so, and others are either frauds or just not very good. Here are some guidelines to follow.

The best way to find a medium is through recommendations from friends or family members who have actually gone to the medium and were impressed. If you can't find a medium that way, you might visit a New Age bookstore and ask for recommendations. Some such shops have back rooms where psychics and mediums give readings. If you're interested in contacting a lost loved one, make sure you ask for a medium, not a psychic card reader. Find out if the manager or clerk knows anyone who has had a reading with the recommended medium. Follow through and talk to the person. Ask how good the medium was on connecting with lost loved ones or deceased friends.

Avoid gypsy palm readers who advertise with large signs in the front of buildings along busy commercial streets. Typically, they offer a similar reading to everyone who comes their way and attempt to get clients to pay additional fees for psychic protection, to cast a love spell or curse, or other manipulations aimed at creating an expensive dependence.

When you find a medium, don't pay an exorbitant fee. You should be able to get a reading that lasts thirty to forty minutes from a capable medium for no more than seventy dollars. Don't provide any information to the medium during at least the first half of the reading. However, don't sit there with your arms crossed and your energy centers shut down, either.

What kind of information is provided? Note how accurate and detailed it is. If someone from the other side comes through, are you able to identify who it is? Are you given any meaningful personal messages? In the final ten or fifteen minutes, you might want to ask questions. Keep in mind the reader is now able to gather information about you based on your questions. However, sometimes it's worthwhile to provide the medium with direction in order to find out what you are seeking.

Practice 28: Analyzing a Medium

While our emphasis in this book is on self-help and making contact with the other side on your own, many of us who are interested in the realm of spirit contact occasionally seek out the aid of a medium. If you've done so yourself, write down in your journal what you remember from a reading or consult your notes to help you analyze the reading. Jot down the main points you were told, and consider the following questions.

Did you know the medium before the reading? How much did he or she know about you? How much did you tell the medium about yourself prior to or during the reading? Did the reader describe the loved one you were hoping to contact in an accurate way, or was it a general description that could fit many people?

What did the reader pick up about your past, your current situation, and your future? How specific were the comments? Regarding future events, did any of them come true yet? Did the predictions relate to your life and seem like reasonable possibilities?

Did the medium claim to make contact with a deceased loved one? If so, how did the medium describe the spirit's relationship to you? Was a name or initial provided? Did you recognize whom the medium was referring to? What message came through? Was it a general message of love and an assurance that everything was well on the other side? Or did the medium provide any specifics that convinced you the contact was genuine?

How did you feel about the reading? Did you come away with a sense that contact with the other side had been made? Or was it too general, a reading that might fit almost anyone?

Rate your reading on a scale of one to ten. Learn from the experience, but don't become dependent on readings to contact the other side. You can make contact yourself.

10

❁

Trickster
Spirits & More

WHEN WE ARE simply going about our lives—tending to our families, working, building careers—spirits can make themselves known in ways both large and small. Sometimes, they do this through mischievous antics—the way of the trickster.

Poet Sharlie West had known for years that her house was haunted. She had gotten used to the spirits, which tended to be more active when the house was filled with children. Items would mysteriously disappear and never be found. Noises without apparent cause could be heard at odd hours of the day and night. Everyone in the family kidded about it.

"One Thanksgiving the family was sitting around the table talking about our occasional spirit visitors," she wrote us in an e-mail. "We were drinking wine and gave a Thanksgiving toast, raising our glasses high. Someone said, 'If there are any ghosts, let them make themselves known.' We were all smiling until her (the toaster's) wine glass broke midair into tiny pieces and splattered all over the table. Dead silence after that. I got chills realizing that although we kidded about the spirits, they were definitely there."

In mythology, the archetype of the trickster, like Loki and Hermes, plays among the gods and through his cunning and trickery becomes a god. He's neither good nor bad but represents the unpredictability of life, the ability to surprise and confuse. He's a rebel who refuses to conform, is loyal to no one, manipulates circumstances, and bends the rules. In legend, the trickster is often depicted as a fox, a raven, a rabbit, or a coyote, who tricks us by not playing by the rules. Irony and a dark wryness are his calling cards.

The Sméagol/Gollum character in Tolkien's *The Lord of the Rings* is the personification of the archetype. He's a mischievous hobbit imp who, as Sméagol, was corrupted by the ring and whose life as Gollum was so prolonged that by the time he met Bilbo Baggins, he had descended into madness.

In the Batman comic books and movies, the trickster is, of course, the Joker. Since the Joker's inception in 1940, his character has gone through various permutations. Initially, he was depicted as a super villain and his origin was kept purposefully vague. By 2008, with *The Dark Knight Rises,* when Heath Ledger played the role, the Joker had become a force of nature.

Synchronicities that Reveal
the Powerful Archetype of Death

There are instances where the trickster archetype seems to work through our individual souls or spirits to make a final wry statement:

- Will Rogers, humorist, actor, and writer, died in a plane crash with his aviator buddy, Wiley Post, shortly after taking off from a lagoon in Point Barrow, Alaska. Rogers's typewriter was found in the debris, a piece of paper rolled into it, and the last word he typed was *death.* Even Rogers probably got a kick out of that one.

- Hours after famed Trappist monk Thomas Merton proclaimed in an important meeting with religious leaders that the times ahead were *electrifying,* he died by electrocution while sitting in the bathtub.

- Jim Fixx, whose 1977 bestseller, *The Complete Book of Running,* triggered the jogging craze, died of a heart attack while running. The irony here, of course, is that Fixx's soul decided to depart while he was doing what he enjoyed. Is there any better way to go?

- James Heselden, who bought the Segway company, died when he drove his Segway over a thirty-foot cliff on his property and into the river below. In this story, as in the Fixx example, the trickster grabs our attention through irony and prompts us to question the nature of our beliefs.

Some trickster archetypes seem to be the voice of a person's soul or spirit providing a glimpse of the future:

- The last movie that John Huston directed before his death was called *The Dead.*

- The last book of poetry that Anne Sexton published before she committed suicide in 1974 was entitled *The Death Notebooks.*

- At the time of his death, Philip K. Dick was working on a novel entitled *The Owl in Daylight.* In esoteric traditions, the owl is considered a messenger between the living and the dead.

- The last song that Hank Williams wrote was "Angel of Death." When he died, he had a hit single at the top of the charts: "I'll Never Get Out of This World Alive."

The night before Sugar Ray Robinson fought Jimmy Doyle in 1947, he dreamed he killed his opponent with a single left hook. According to ESPN's Larry Schwartz, Robinson was so shaken by the dream that the next morning he said he couldn't fight Doyle. The promoters, who would lose money if the fight was cancelled, brought in a Catholic priest who told Robinson not to worry about his dream. Robinson knocked out Doyle in the eighth round. Doyle was carried from the ring on a stretcher and died the next day.

These types of synchronicities underscore the power of the archetype we call death. "An archetype is like a natural force," wrote Robert Hopcke in *There Are No Accidents*. It can be as powerful as a tornado, whipping into our lives, creating chaos.

It's likely at some point in your life, a trickster spirit has pulled some fast ones on you. It might be something as simple as the proverbial missing sock you're certain went into the washer or the dryer, but never came out. Or the whereabouts of your keys, wallet, or a particular book or file. Around our house, we refer to this phenomenon as the mysterious black hole where all sorts of things vanish mysteriously.

During the Christmas holidays one year, we were in the kitchen and Trish mentioned she needed some cash and would head over to the bank the next day. Rob said she didn't need to, he had cash, and held out a hundred dollar bill. Her hands were full at that moment—opening cat food or dog food—and she asked him to set it down.

He put the bill on top of a container of raw almonds and Trish went about her business. When she turned around, the bill was gone. "Hey, Rob? Did you put that bill down?"

"On the almond container," he called from his office.

"It's not there."

"Of course it's there."

But it wasn't. We searched in the obvious places. The almond container was close to the edge of the counter and the trash can was right under it. We went through every gross item in the trash bag, searched the silverware drawer, the cabinets, went through the garbage again. We cast accusing looks at the cats, the dog. The bill was gone.

We concluded a trickster spirit might be stirring up mischief.

In another instance, Rob called someone for an interview to try to gain some particular knowledge. But the subject was apparently unwilling to cooperate. No response was ever received from his attempts. When no interview was forthcoming, he let it go.

Four months after the last attempt, he and Trish found themselves in a bar-restaurant seated at the same high-top table as the man he had wanted to interview. Amazingly, they were both in a city that neither lived in. A live band was playing and it was difficult to talk at length, but the man was agreeable after meeting Rob and gave him his e-mail address.

It was an incredibly meaningful coincidence. But it turned into a trickster synchronicity when Rob was unable to find the scrap of paper containing the e-mail address. The interview was lost again, and it seemed the trickster was at play.

PRACTICE 29: YOUR TRICKSTER EXPERIENCE

Think back to times when something similar happened to you. Did it involve a mysterious disappearance of an object or objects? Was it something else such as a glass or other object breaking for no reason? Maybe a picture repeatedly fell off the wall. Maybe it was something you really wanted, but when you got the result it was a nightmare. The possibilities are endless.

- What were the circumstances?

- Were there other similar instances around this time?

- What was the mood in your living environment or wherever the incident happened?

- Was there a pattern to the incidents?

The Monk in the Singing Bowl

One December several years ago, Trish ordered a singing bowl from Theresa, a woman who travels to Thailand once a year to purchase genuine articles made by local artisans. At the time Trish ordered the bowl, she and Theresa talked about what kind of bowl might be appropriate for Rob. She asked Trish some questions about him, then said she would try out some bowls for tones and pick one she intuitively felt would fit him. She also mentioned that sometimes these ancient bowls are accompanied by the spirits of the monks who owned them. Trish thought it would be kind of cool, a monk sharing our space.

After Christmas, Rob started using the bowl at the end of his yoga classes, invoking a rich, sonorous sound that brings you out of a relaxed state and back into the real world. Throughout January, Trish kept waiting for the spirit of the monk to show up.

One day we got home from the gym and found the French doors that face the back porch wide open. Yet Trish knew she had shut and locked the doors before they'd left. It went on like this for several days—doors that were locked, things missing that were in plain sight, a kind of trickster twist. For instance, the key that had been in the lock on the inside door of the cabana bathroom since we bought the house more than a decade earlier was now missing. We didn't even know this key could be pulled out of the lock, that's how permanent it seemed. But it was gone.

And then the missing hundred dollar bill mentioned earlier. That was when Trish began to suspect the spirit of the monk who had owned the singing bowl was around and that he was a trickster. There had also been a shift in energies in the house. Two of the three cats we had at the time were female and used to despise each other. They stopped squabbling. The stray cat we were feeding at the time strolled in and out of the house and none of the other cats cared. We slept better at night. We trusted in a benevolent universe.

Trish wrote Theresa about the strange disappearances that she attributed to this trickster spirit of the monk. Theresa replied with a story about how once a woman returned one of the singing bowls she'd bought because it was inhabited by three spectral monks.

We didn't have three monks, but we felt sure we had at least one. We formally invited him out of the shadows to make himself known, and asked that he stop disappearing objects.

We never found the hundred dollar bill. But seven years after that key vanished, Trish found it in some stones just outside the cabana bathroom door. The only reason she saw it was because the stones had been moved around by a dog chasing lizards. The spirit of the monk doesn't seem to be around anymore. Perhaps he approves of Rob's use of his singing bowl, that beautiful music that rises up after each yoga class and suffuses our souls, bringing harmony and peace.

Trickster Spirits in the Oddest Places

These mischievous spirits can make themselves known anywhere, at any time, through any means. You can readily identify them through their wry irony and the sometimes-dark mischief or malign intent they perpetrate. But they are also identifiable by their goofy antics and the lengths they'll often go to in order to make their presence known.

During Trish's last year in college, she lived in a small apartment on the third floor of an old building in upstate New York. She and her roommate, Martha, shared their cramped living space with a tabby cat. Early in the school year, Martha's grandmother passed away.

One day not long afterward, Martha's mother found a straight pin on the gravestone where Martha's grandmother was buried. A few days later, Trish's tabby, Tigger, was about to jump into a chair where Trish was reading and suddenly did a 180-degree spin in midair and tore into the bedroom. Martha and Trish looked at each other, wondering what *that* was about.

The next morning, Trish found straight pins scattered around the living room—a pin stuck in a couch cushion, pins lying on the rug, a couple more straight pins on the kitchen table. This began to happen consistently. When Martha mentioned it to her mother, she laughed and said it was Martha's grandmother. "Nana loved to sew. I've been finding straight pins all over the house, even underlining passages in the Bible." Trish and Martha suspected Tigger had seen Nana about the time the straight pins appeared. But how did a ghost manipulate physical matter, even matter as small as a straight pin? One weekend when they visited Martha's parents, her mother showed them the straight pins underlining passages in the Bible. The straight pin phenomenon continued consistently for several months, then gradually stopped.

A few years later, Trish met Martha and her mother in St. Augustine and they visited one of the best-known tourist sites—Castillo de San Marcos. It was built in 1672, when Florida was part of the Spanish empire, to protect the city of St. Augustine. Today it's the oldest masonry fort in the US. It's made of coquina rock, composed of small seashells, and when you touch it, you can feel the tiny shells, their odd shapes, long bleached white from the sun. Rocks hold energy, and given the history of the fort, that energy is conducive to spirit contact.

In November 1702, the British attacked St. Augustine and the Castillo de San Marcos, and during the two-month siege, 1,200 Spanish civilians and 300 soldiers remained in the fort. The British were unable to take it over, and the Spanish claimed victory. However, before the British left, they burned most of the town to the ground.

In 1740, the Brits again tried to take the fort by starving the Spanish civilians and soldiers inside. That siege lasted twenty-seven days—until the British retreated because they ran out of food and supplies. The fort never fell to the opposition in battle and the Brits took control only after the Treaty of Paris was signed in 1763. The darker part of the fort's story started in 1875, when it was used as a prison for Native Americans taken captive in the West. Its prisoners included the famous Seminole chief Osceola, who died within three months of his captivity.

As Trish, Martha, and her mother moved through the empty hallways, their footsteps echoed against the ancient coquina rock. The whisper of the past was everywhere. But everything was bare—the thick walls, the well-worn floors, not even a piece of trash in sight. They were talking about finding the cell where Osceola was held and marveling that in spite of the summer heat outside, the interior of the fort was cool and pleasant. Trish happened to look down and stopped, incredulous, staring at a single straight pin on that bare coquina floor. She picked it up and showed it to Martha's mother. "What're the odds of finding a straight pin in this place?" she asked.

Martha's mother smiled. "I've been feeling Nana around."

"Looks like she wanted to tour the place with us," Martha said.

The circumstances are stunning. Simple straight pins, the tools a seamstress used throughout her life, are found in the homes of her daughter and granddaughter in the days and months following her death. A decade later, a single straight pin is found in the empty hallway of an old, haunted fort while they are touring the fort with the granddaughter's friend, who also experienced the same straight pins.

The trickster element here is tiered: the object of contact is the same, but is found in a location where it's highly unlikely you'd see a straight pin; the three people involved in the initial contact are together several years later; all of them recognize the significance of the event and comment on it. And the message seems to be, *Hey, I'm still around, watching out for you.*

PRACTICE 30: IDENTIFYING A TRICKSTER EVENT

When you had an experience with a trickster spirit, how did you react? Which questions apply to you?

1. Were you angry, confused, frustrated, or upset? Did you rail against the universe for being cruel and unfair? Do you still feel that way? Do you live with the loss as a permanent condition, like a widow who only wears black in public?

2. Were you temporarily sad and at a loss? Did you gradually accept the changed circumstances and adapt to a new reality?

3. Were people you know surprised by how quickly you moved on from the event? Do you see a larger picture or higher order behind the events?

PRACTICE 31: HOW DID YOU RELATE TO THE TRICKSTER ELEMENT?

1. It was ironic, but not something I ever thought about.

2. It was on my mind for a long time. I still think about it and wonder what it means.

3. The trickster element is proof to me the universe can be cruel and dangerous.

4. The trickster woke me up to the larger picture and my place in it.

5. I can see how some people might think the trickster is a demon, but I learned a valuable lesson and moved on.

Conclusion

Spirits communicate with us in a variety of ways, shapes, and forms, as we've shown. Hopefully, you recognize the veil between our physical world and the afterlife is thin and it's possible to reach through from either side!

The key is to tune in to the means of communication. As we've seen, spirits seem to use almost anything available to them to get our attention. Some of the common methods are loud noises, shattered glass, music and songs, words that appear on fogged glass, objects, numbers, names, clouds, animals, birds, and even insects. In most instances, synchronicity is a vital component of spirit contact, because such meaningful coincidences raise our antennas and expand our awareness. Sometimes the communication is direct, as in a voice or an ethereal image. But often it is felt rather than seen or heard. It's subtle and requires you to pay attention.

For some of us, it's easier and safer to simply ignore these experiences, to write them off as random coincidences. Skeptics tend to dismiss spiritual communication as wishful thinking, a silly hope that the consciousness of the deceased is still alive somewhere. After all, mainstream science says there's no proof of life after death, only anecdotes, which aren't considered evidence. Yet when the anecdotes are our own personal experiences, we gain a profound richness and wonder that comes from spirit contact. And our experiences ultimately provide us with the real proof, the only proof that really matters.

"We each have a choice about how to engage with these unique human capabilities and mysterious forces, which lie hidden behind the façade of our material world. They have the power to redefine who we are, and to change our perception of life and death," wrote Leslie Kean in *Surviving Death: A Journalist Investigates Evidence for an Afterlife.*[46]

When these experiences are initiated from the other side, they tend to surprise, comfort, and even energize us, especially when they occur in clusters. But interaction with spirits is a two-way street. We can stimulate contact ourselves through focused meditation and by incubating our dreams. But also by watching for signs and symbols appearing in our everyday lives. Sometimes contact comes during meditation without you making any effort. When you're quiet, you're more receptive.

When we actively engage in spirit communication, we may tap into what physicist David Bohm called the *implicate order* or *enfolded reality*, a kind of primal soup that births everything in the universe, even space and time. [47] If so, then within this implicate order, death is merely a transition from one form to another and communication with the deceased is not only possible, but is accessible to everyone.

When Rob leads meditations during his yoga classes, he often asks students to connect with their true selves, which is separate from the mind chatter or internal dialogue that tends to disrupt meditation. But where is that true self? How do we connect with it? It could be that our true self can be found on the so-called other side—Bohm's enfolded reality.

---

46   Leslie Kean. *Surviving Death: A Journalist Investigates Evidence for an Afterlife.* (New York: Crown), 362.

47   Michael Talbot. *The Holographic Universe: The Revolutionary Theory of Reality.* (New York: Harper Perennial, 2011), 46.S.

If that's the case, the spirit world is our natural home, and the physical world and our flesh-and-bone existence is a projection of that realm.

Considering this close connection, it could be that our decisions influence spirits and their desires influence our lives. If so, reality is a whole lot stranger and more complex than we have been taught to believe. However, if we can learn the basics of deciphering the essence of spirit contact, we can better comprehend the interplay between worlds and make use of our fluency to improve our lives and the lives of others.

Resources

Alvarez, Melissa. *Animal Frequency: Identify, Attune, and Connect to the Energy of Animals.* Woodbury, MN: Llewellyn, 2017.

Andrews, Ted. *Animal Speak: The Spiritual & Magical Powers of Creatures Great & Small.* St. Paul, MN: Llewellyn, 2002.

Bair, Deirdre. *Jung: A Biography.* New York: Little, Brown Company, 2003.

Beitman, Bernard D. *Connecting with Coincidence: The New Science for Using Synchronicity and Serendipity in Your Life.* Deerfield Beach, FL: HCI Books, 2016.

Cameron, W. Bruce. *A Dog's Purpose: A Novel for Humans.* New York: Forge Books, 2016.

Hopcke, Robert. *There Are No Accidents: Synchronicity and the Stories of Our Lives.* New York: Macmillan, 1997.

Ingerman, Sandra. *Shamanic Journeying: A Beginner's Guide.* Louisville, CO: Sounds True, 2008.

Lindbergh, Charles A. *Autobiography of Values*. New York: Harcourt Brace Jovanovich, 1978.

MacGregor, Rob. *Jewel in the Lotus: Meditation for Busy Minds*. Hertford, NC: Crossroad Press, 2015

MacGregor, Trish, and Millie Germondo. *Animal Totems: The Power and Prophecy of Your Animal Guides*. Hertford, NC: Fair Winds Press, 2004.

MacGregor, Trish, and Rob MacGregor. *Synchronicity and the Other Side: Your Guide to Meaningful Connections with the Afterlife*. Avon, MA: Adams Media, 2011.

MacGregor, Trish, and Rob MacGregor. *The 7 Secrets of Synchronicity: Your Guide to Finding Meaning in Signs Big and Small*. Avon, MA: Adams Media, 2011.

Martin, Joel, and Patricia Romanowski. *Love Beyond Life: The Healing Power of After-Death Communications*. New York: Harper, 1997.

Miller, Sukie. *After Death: How People Around the World Map the Journey After Life*. New York: Simon & Schuster, 1998.

Monroe, Robert. *Journeys Out of the Body: The Classic Work on Out-of-Body Experience*. New York: Broadway Books, 1992.

Moody, Raymond. *Life After Life: The Bestselling Original Investigation that Revealed "Near-Death Experiences."* New York: HarperOne, 2015.

Moody, Raymond. *Paranormal: My Life in Pursuit of the Afterlife*. New York: HarperOne, 2013.

Noory, George, and Guiley, Rosemary Ellen. *Talking to the Dead*. New York: Forge Books, 2011.

Stevenson, Ian. *Twenty Cases Suggestive of Reincarnation: Second Edition, Revised and Enlarged.* Charlottesville, VA: University of Virginia Press, 1980.

Tarnas, Richard. *Cosmos and Psyche: Intimations of a New World View.* New York: Penguin Group, 2006.

Wilson, Colin. *Poltergeist: A Study in Destructive Haunting.* New York: Putnam, 1981.

To Write the Authors

If you wish to contact the authors or would like more information about this book, please write to the authors in care of Llewellyn Worldwide, and we will forward your request. Both the authors and publisher appreciate hearing from you and learning of your enjoyment of this book and how it has helped you. Llewellyn Worldwide cannot guarantee that every letter written to the authors can be answered, but all will be forwarded. Please write to:

Trish MacGregor and Rob MacGregor
℅ Llewellyn Worldwide
2143 Wooddale Drive
Woodbury, MN 55125-2989

Please enclose a self-addressed stamped envelope for reply,
or $1.00 to cover costs. If outside the USA, enclose
an international postal reply coupon.